EYEWITNESS ◉ GUIDES

ARCHAEOLOGY

MAR 2000

AUCHTERDERRAN

PRIMARY/SEN RESOURCES

Small brush

Measuring tape

Iron slave manacles from Roman Britain, 1st–2nd century A.D.

Sample of peat

Half-conserved bronze bowl, United Arab Emirates, 1st century A.D.

Bronze manicure set from Roman London, 2nd century A.D.

Lion perfume vase from Etruscan Italy, c. 300 B.C.

Stone mould with bronze chisel and large flat axe

Animal bones showing
butcher's marks

Stucco head from
Central Asia,
7th–8th century A.D.

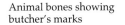
EYEWITNESS GUIDES

ARCHAEOLOGY

Written by
DR JANE McINTOSH

Sherds of spouted
"hole-mouth" jar
from an Early Bronze
Age olive oil factory
in Jordan, c. 2000 B.C.

Hand pick

Trowel

Forgery of shabti
figure placed in
Egyptian tombs to
care for the dead
in the afterlife

Photo
scale

DK
DORLING KINDERSLEY
London • New York • Stuttgart

Cast-iron
hands, an
example of
industrial
archaeology

A DORLING KINDERSLEY BOOK

Project editor Marion Dent
Art editor Vicky Wharton
Managing editor Simon Adams
Managing art editor Julia Harris
Research Céline Carez
Picture research Miriam Sharland
Production Catherine Semark
Special photography Geoff Brightling

This Eyewitness ® Guide has been conceived by
Dorling Kindersley Limited
and Editions Gallimard

First published in Great Britain in 1994 by
Dorling Kindersley Limited,
9 Henrietta Street, London WC2E 8PS

· 4 6 8 10 9 7 5 3 ·

Copyright © 1994 Dorling Kindersley Limited, London
Text copyright © 1994 Jane McIntosh

http://www.dk.com

All rights reserved. No part of this
publication may be reproduced, stored in
a retrieval system, or transmitted in any
form or by any means, electronic, mechanical,
photocopying, recording or otherwise, without
the prior written permission of the copyright owner.

A CIP catalogue record for this book is
available from the British Library.

ISBN 0 7513 6032 5

Typesetting by Litho Link Ltd,
Welshpool, Powys
Colour reproduction by Colourscan, Singapore
Printed in China by Toppan Printing Co., (Shenzhen) Ltd

Roman amphora
for storing olive oil

Twentieth-century copy of a
Visigothic gold eagle brooch
of the 6th century A.D.

Three coins of
Roman empero[r]
Claudius – real,
contemporary
forgery, and
modern forgery

Stucco head,
5th century A.D.,
found in deserts
of Central Asia

Black-glazed
drinking vessel
from Etruscan Italy,
4th century B.C.

Contents

Bronze
cauldron from
Sutton Hoo

Detecting the past

WHAT IS ARCHAEOLOGY? The actual word comes from the Greek and means "the study of what is ancient". It is the past seen from a human perspective. Archaeologists, palaeontologists, and historians are all interested in the past, but their viewpoints are different. Palaeontologists study fossilized remains, while historians deal with written records – the "conscious" past. For archaeologists, fossil and documentary findings are only two of many sources of information. Archaeologists deal with all the information we can obtain about the past from material remains – evidence that is generally biased and incomplete, but whose scope is almost unlimited.

"Lucy", an unusually complete fossil skeleton of the earliest species directly ancestral to us – *Australopithecus afarensis*

Sacrum connecting spine to pelvis

Female pelvis

Details of Lucy's skeleton, such as a thigh bone, show that she walked upright

HOW OLD IS THE HUMAN RACE?
This has been a burning question since Charles Darwin's *Origin of Species* (1859) introduced the concept of evolution. To discover the remains of our earliest ancestors takes an inspired selection of the right location and good luck. Hominids (human ancestral species) like Lucy were not numerous. Major geological changes or natural disasters such as volcanoes and earthquakes had to occur before their fossilized remains were exposed.

"YOU CAN'T TAKE IT WITH YOU"
Many past societies believed that you could, equipping the dead with everything they would need in the afterlife. This fluted, Byzantine silver bowl from the Sutton Hoo burial illustrates all that is spectacular in archaeology. Made in the Eastern Mediterranean, it found its way to England and was deliberately placed as a funerary offering in the rich ship burial of a king (pp. 26–27). Valuable, exotic, luxurious objects like this reflect not only the status of the owner, but also the long-distance links between societies, their prosperity, and their beliefs.

SURPRISE!
Archaeologists are interested in every aspect of life. It is surprising how much information, particularly about diet and health, can be gained from toilets, like this one from England's Viking York. People accidentally drop in personal possessions, but rarely retrieve them! Rubbish thrown into cesspits is invaluable in reconstructing people's lives.

Preserved oak leaf from the *Mary Rose* (pp. 32–35)

LIVING IN THE PAST
Today archaeologists are interested in the whole way of life of people in the past, including the landscape which they inhabited. Plant remains, from charred grains and pollen to this oak leaf from the *Mary Rose*, provide evidence of past vegetation. This is supplemented by clues from snails and other minibeasts. Now we can begin to see not only what the world looked like in the past, but also how people have changed it.

Face is off-centre, showing how carelessly bowl was crafted

CHILDREN'S PLAYTHINGS
Much of the excitement of the past lies in its rich diversity, but it is also fascinating to see how similar people are from culture to culture and from age to age. These two rag dolls lie 2,000 years apart, but the children who owned them must have had many feelings and games in common.

Much-loved rag doll from Roman-occupied Egypt, early A.D.

Rag doll "Columbia" personifies 1890s' USA

Leather sandals, Britain, 2nd century A.D.

A STEP BACK IN TIME
Burials were deliberate and monuments were erected to endure. But most material from which archaeologists reconstruct the past was preserved by accident, as when a house collapsed, preserving all contents in their place. More commonly, archaeologists find house foundations with rubbish on the floor or thrown into pits. Other discoveries are of objects accidentally lost. Inorganic materials (pottery and stone tools) predominate, but occasionally organic remains, like these leather sandals, survive.

Silver bowl – a rich offering in grave of Raedwald, High King of England, c. A.D. 625

STANDING STONES
The most striking ancient remains are monuments, such as England's Stonehenge (left) or Mexico's Olmec heads (pp. 12–13). But how were they built and why? We may gain some understanding of the technology and manpower involved in erecting such monuments, but the reasons why may baffle us forever.

Preservation and decay

LITTLE OF THE PAST SURVIVES. Only a fraction of the things used in a person's lifetime ends up in the ground – objects that are lost, thrown away, or deliberately buried. Of these, only a few survive. Some decay naturally, others are physically destroyed, and the chances of survival decrease as time passes. Of the surviving fraction, only a very small proportion is likely to be rediscovered and even less of what is uncovered is properly recorded and preserved. It is from this tiny fraction that archaeologists attempt to reconstruct the past. This means that we know a great deal more about some aspects of life than others.

Pleated cloth from royal tomb, Assyria, 8th century B.C.

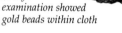

X-ray examination showed gold beads within cloth

MAKING AN IMPRESSION
Textiles and other organic materials only survive in exceptional conditions. Sometimes they survive as impressions on objects or in soil, as did this cloth, but ancient clothing is mainly known from art.

MADE OF METAL
Ancient gold and silver survive well, but copper and bronze can suffer surface corrosion. Iron rusts, and may be completely destroyed. Scientific examination of shapeless metal lumps reveals the original appearance, which may be restored by conservation.

Iron socketed axe, Britain, c. 7th– 6th century B.C.

BUILDING MATERIALS
Usually wooden buildings survive only as postholes. Durable building stone is often robbed for reuse. Mounds developed where successive brick structures were levelled and new ones built. Abandoned stone or brick settlements, like Pakistan's great 4000-year-old Mohenjo Daro, have often survived.

Lotus flower design

BOTTOMS UP!
Pottery is about the most common find from archaeological sites worldwide from the last 10,000 years. Although easily broken, there are few environments where broken pieces will not survive indefinitely. Vessels made of other materials are much less commonly found. Usually they were less durable, and often more expensive, so they were treasured and in shorter supply. Glass degenerates in many soils, while containers of leather, wood, or plant materials rarely survive.

One of the earliest examples of Roman blown glass, 1st century A.D.

Simple red ware pottery bowl from the Neolithic, Ukraine, 3700–3000 B.C.

Lotus cup from Egypt, c. 1250 B.C., made of faience – a blue-glazed mixture of sand and soda fired just below melting point (850°C, 1562°F)

Skull from
Herculaneum in
Italy preserved
in ash

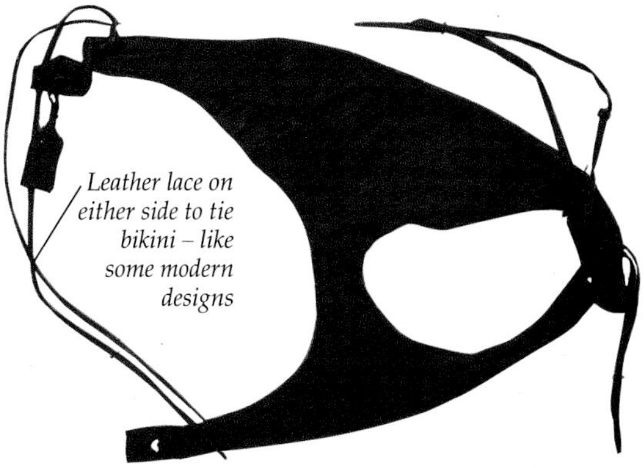

*Leather lace on
either side to tie
bikini – like
some modern
designs*

BARELY DECENT

Fashions do not always change with
the passing of time – this modern-looking leather
bikini bottom is nearly 2000 years old! It has
survived because it found its way into a timber-
lined well in Roman London, where waterlogging
prevented its decay. Wells are a rich source of
organic remains of all kinds. In complete contrast, so
too are dry environments such as caves in highland
Mexico or the pueblos of southwest USA.

HEAD-HUNTING

The survival of human remains is very
variable. Many soils preserve bones, so
skeletons are the most common find, but in acid
peatbogs bones may disappear while skin, hair,
and insides survive. The body may completely
disappear and still be detectable – like Sutton
Hoo sand bodies (pp. 42–43) or Pompeii's
lava moulds (pp. 28–29). In completely arid
environments desiccated bodies are
found, while "deep-freeze"
conditions can ensure perfect
preservation (pp. 30–31).

Ancient
Egyptian mummy

*Blue glass
with thin
threads of
white glass
decoration*

Drinking horn
from kingdom of the
Lombards, northern
Italy, 6th century A.D.

*Staves made
from narrow
pieces of
wood bound
round with
wooden
bands –
designed to
hold liquids*

Wooden drinking
vessel used by a soldier
or sailor aboard the *Mary
Rose*, which sank in 1545

Underground

Hᴏᴡ ᴅᴏᴇs ᴛʜᴇ ᴘᴀsᴛ get under the ground? The ground level gradually rises over the years, burying the past beneath it. Layer upon layer of decaying vegetation, rocks and hill soils eroded by weather and rivers, demolished buildings, and rubbish thrown down on the street – all pile up in horizontal layers, the oldest layers at the bottom, the most recent at the top. These may be disturbed by natural disasters such as earthquakes, or by people digging holes. The process of horizontal deposition, known as stratification, is vital in dating the past.

BLOW OUT
Volcanic eruptions dramatically bury the past. The eruption of Santorini in the Aegean Sea, c. 1500 B.C., completely blew out the centre of the island, burying the surviving land under volcanic deposits in which remains of beautifully painted Minoan houses were entombed.

SQUALID DWELLINGS
Layers of deposits develop rapidly in towns. The earth floors of these houses in England 's Viking York (Jorvik) rose as mud came in on shoes, while food waste and other debris were thrown on the floor. The wattle-walled houses were often repaired or rebuilt, always at a slightly higher level to match the constantly rising street level.

WELL-FLATTENED
The way deposits accumulate depends partly on how the remains decay. The Sutton Hoo ship burial (pp. 26–27) was covered in sand, preserving details of its decayed timbers. But in the central wooden chamber, sand was kept out until the roof collapsed, by which time many objects had decayed. Those remaining were scattered by the roof fall, and many were crushed.

Part of a superb sheet bronze cauldron crushed flat when the roof collapsed

Roman pit cut away by medieval pit

A SLICE THROUGH TIME
A section through part of the 2,000-year-old city of London illustrates the constant rise in urban levels through time. The ground level at various periods can be established by looking at floors. From these levels, features were dug – mostly cesspits – which cut through earlier floor levels and deposits. Between floors, debris accumulated in subsequent years, or was deliberately shovelled in to level the ground before rebuilding. The rate of development accelerated over recent centuries.

Brick-lined well, c. 1800, covered by 19th-century concrete floor, cut down to natural soil

17th-century tiled floor

Late 16th-century ground level

19th-century drain, cutting earlier floor

19th-century concrete foundations cutting through all deposits down to natural soil

19th-century level

18th-century level

17th-century level

14th- to 15th-century chalk floor, cut by later features

Late 16th-century chalk-lined cesspit cuts through Roman and medieval floors

Anglo-Saxon posthole

Roman ground level, A.D. 1st to 2nd century

1st-century pit, capped by 1st-2nd century Roman tiled floor

SIX FEET UNDER
Usually the past gets underground by accident, but sometimes burial is deliberate: valuables hidden in troubled times, or people buried in simple graves or elaborate tombs. The tomb of Egyptian pharaoh, Tutankhamun, survived the usual ancient tomb robbing, to be dramatically rediscovered by Howard Carter (1874–1939) in 1922.

BRAVING THE ELEMENT
Intrepid explorers Stephens and Catherwood rediscovered the Maya civilization in inhospitable jungle. Luxuriant vegetation, numerous insects, and tropical climate make jungles a rapid destroyer of antiquities, but also protect them against looters.

Looking at the landscape

MODERN ARCHAEOLOGISTS look not just at ancient dwellings but at the whole landscape used by humans – fields, pastures, and woodlands associated with settlements and traces of early people's widespread activities. Unlike excavation, survey methods used to investigate these large areas are cheap and rapid. But not everything that lies under the ground can be detected from above. Material, such as pot-sherds or brick, scattered on the surface indicates that there could be features buried below which are being disturbed, particularly by ploughing. The most recent features, lying close to the ground's surface, are the most likely to produce such evidence, while earlier ones may remain undisturbed. Aerial reconnaissance, remote sensing, and geophysical survey can detect some things better than others, so they give only a partial picture of what lies under the ground.

LYING AROUND
You do not need to dig to discover the past. Field walking involves the systematic collection, recording, and mapping of material lying on the surface. It allows settlements and other buried activity areas to be identified and dated.

"MOON BUGGY"
Geophysical survey equipment, using radar, echo-sounding, electrical resistivity, or magnetic variation, picks up variations in the soil that reflect buried features. Different machines can "see" to different depths and detect different things. However, their results must be interpreted carefully.

Modern field boundary

Field of winter wheat is riper (and so paler) over buried ditches

Modern pipeline trench

Now dry watercourse flowed in Roman times

Roman linear settlement – ditches acted like garden fences around Roman buildings

Modern ditch

Recently dug stream

Modern track follows line of medieval track, dividing blocks of medieval fields

Perimeter of Iron Age enclosure, with ditch and internal bank

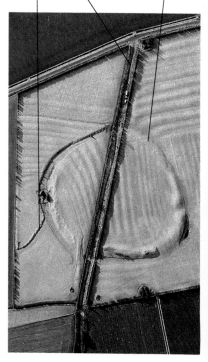

SNAKING ACROSS THE LANDSCAPE
Enduring structures such as mounds are the surviving stubs of ancient landscapes. Isolated churches in England, for example, are often the only surviving buildings from villages deserted in medieval times. The Serpent Mound in Ohio, USA (above) was a religious monument built by the Adena people. It is a visible relic of a landscape that originally included burials and villages.

CROP MARKS FROM THE AIR
The vital water available to growing plants is reduced by such buried obstructions as walls and increased by buried holes, such as ditches. Plants germinate sooner, grow taller, and ripen earlier over buried holes. The patterns of such differences in growth are clearly visible from the air. This photo shows a Roman peat-cutting settlement in the wet fenlands of eastern England; ovals (bottom right) are modern tractor marks.

AN AERIAL VIEW OF SHADOW SITES
When the sun is low, even slight variations in the ground's surface cast clear shadows best seen from the air – like the different views of a carpet seen by a person and a mouse. Identifying patterns is only the beginning – skill and experience are needed to interpret them. Above is an Iron Age hillfort in eastern England. The horizontal and vertical lines show where strip fields once were; the circles (bottom left) are modern horse troughs.

Helmets, such as this, may have been worn to protect players in Central America's ritual ballgame

Basalt blocks were used for these heads and weighed as much as 34 tonnes

Typical Olmec features

BIG BROTHER IS WATCHING
Colossal heads of basalt are an outstanding creation of the Olmec people (1200–600 B.C.) of Mexico's eastern coast. Heads like the one above were deliberately mutilated and buried and may be portraits of rulers. The Olmecs owed their prosperity to rich soils capable of producing two crops a year. The Olmec people dominated the long-distance trade network which flourished throughout Central America and initiated typical features such as a complicated calendar, advanced astronomy, and the grim religion of Meso-American civilization.

HILLS AND HOLES
It is often possible to map directly abandoned sites which have not been built on later. Bumps and hollows, though clad in vegetation, are visible on the surface of the ground. They give a clear plan of features that once stood there, whose typical forms known from excavation elsewhere allow them to be identified. Laguna de los Cerros' undulating pastures (left) cover typical features of Olmec ceremonial centres – pyramids, plazas, platforms, and ballcourts.

All kinds of documents

In early Chinese writing, each sign represents a word or idea

DOCUMENTS – whether inscriptions, coins, official records, or letters – greatly add to our understanding of the past. They record information that may not exist elsewhere and give us direct access to what people thought in the past. But it is for this very reason that we must be wary. Writing always has a purpose, which means it is often biased. Not all documents are in writing, though. Maps may be purely visual. Important historical material can be conveyed in traditional tales, while place names and language also provide invaluable records.

MAN WITH A DREAM
Oral records are valuable. In the 8th century B.C., Homer wrote the *Iliad*, looking back 400 years to a vanished, but not forgotten, world. Following Homer's clues, Heinrich Schliemann set out to discover Troy in the 1870s (above) – and unexpectedly succeeded.

Inscription too short to give good clues for deciphering

Seal

Impression

Impression

Seal

Bull seal

Bull impression

Inscription revealed by infra-red photography

PUZZLE OF THE INDUS CIVILIZATION
Writing reveals a great deal, so it is tantalizing when we cannot read it. Earliest writing of ancient India and Pakistan may never be deciphered, although scholars have identified its language and found its writing goes from right to left. Seals, with picture and brief inscription, were used on merchandise.

FORESEEING THE FUTURE
Writing began to meet one of two needs – to keep official records, as in Sumer (now southern Iraq), or to deal with religious matters. In China questions to the gods were written on bones (above) which were heated. This caused cracks whose pattern was interpreted to give the answer.

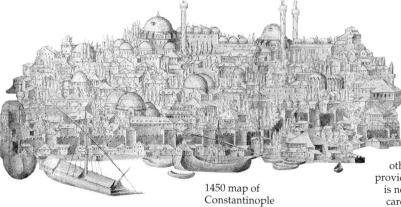

1450 map of Constantinople

FINDING ONE'S WAY AROUND
Archaeological studies of towns or countryside are likely to start with maps. Place names reveal vanished features and the history of settlement locally. Anomalies such as a bend in a hedge line or street layouts show where features such as mounds or city walls have disappeared. Old maps illustrate what has now vanished. But maps, like other documents, may be biased. They provide information for a purpose – what is not relevant may be omitted. So great care is needed when interpreting them.

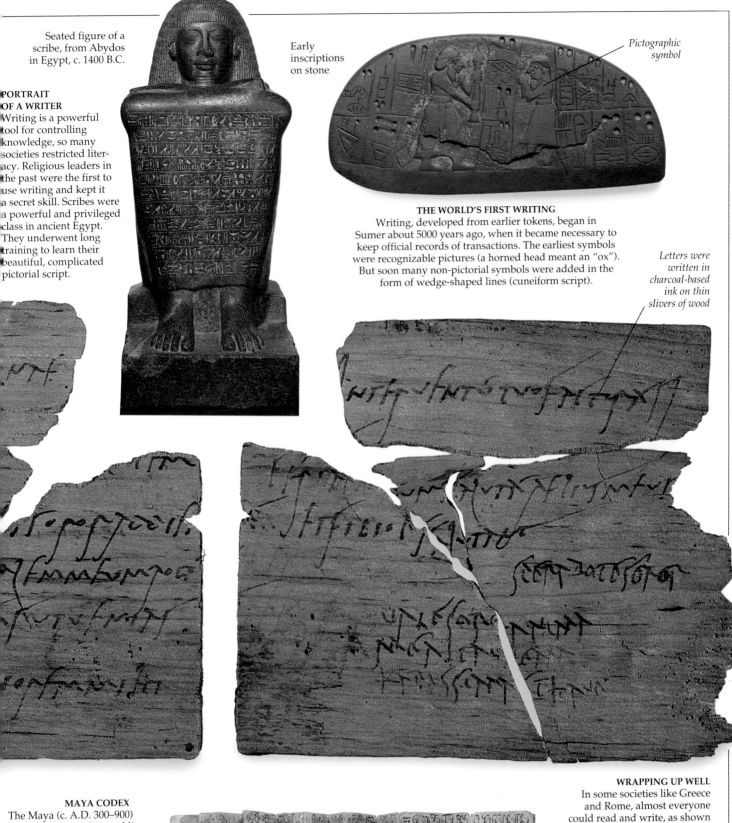

PORTRAIT OF A WRITER

Writing is a powerful tool for controlling knowledge, so many societies restricted literacy. Religious leaders in the past were the first to use writing and kept it a secret skill. Scribes were a powerful and privileged class in ancient Egypt. They underwent long training to learn their beautiful, complicated pictorial script.

Seated figure of a scribe, from Abydos in Egypt, c. 1400 B.C.

Early inscriptions on stone

Pictographic symbol

THE WORLD'S FIRST WRITING

Writing, developed from earlier tokens, began in Sumer about 5000 years ago, when it became necessary to keep official records of transactions. The earliest symbols were recognizable pictures (a horned head meant an "ox"). But soon many non-pictorial symbols were added in the form of wedge-shaped lines (cuneiform script).

Letters were written in charcoal-based ink on thin slivers of wood

MAYA CODEX

The Maya (c. A.D. 300–900) were among the world's greatest mathematicians and astronomers. Their methods of recording dates were extremely complex. They used both a 52-year repeating cycle and historical dates started from 13 August, 3113 B.C. Although many of their texts, like this codex, deal with religious matters, stelae give information about political organization and the warlike activities of their rulers.

WRAPPING UP WELL

In some societies like Greece and Rome, almost everyone could read and write, as shown by the wonderful discovery of letters in the Roman military outpost at Vindolanda in northern England. These range from official military records of stores to chatty correspondence sent to the garrison. One lists winter woollies being sent to a chilly soldier – two pairs of sandals, some woolly socks, and two pairs of underpants!

Images of the past

ART IS NOT ONLY ATTRACTIVE, it is also a window into the past. Paintings and sculptures can show objects such as clothing or wooden architecture that have survived in archaeological sites only as fragments or not at all. Detailed scenes of everyday life, as in ancient Egyptian paintings, show how people lived and how they carried out their work. But art is often symbolic, having a deeper meaning for its creators. Australian Aboriginal paintings depict their mythology, which we cannot understand without their explanations. Without written or verbal information to provide a key, it is hard to unlock the meaning of art.

Mythology and ritual are embodied in Australia's Aboriginal art. The act of repainting can be an integral part of ritual activity.

BUSHMEN'S ROCK ART
Southern Africa's paintings and rock engravings are largely naturalistic, depicting people and animals. Many provide detailed information on hunting practices and equipment. Most of this art is relatively recent, while that of Australia extends very much further back in time. Nevertheless, both form part of a living tradition, telling its makers' stories of the universe and its creation.

THE BEAUTY OF INDIAN ART
The period from 2nd century B.C. to 3rd century A.D. saw the finest flowering of Buddhist art in India, at its peak in the sculptures associated with "stupas" (mounds covering venerated Buddhist cremated remains). Their erection reflects not only religious fervour, but also political and economic prosperity. Amaravati stupa (three slabs of it shown) is perhaps the finest. Although the subject matter is religious, the art style has its roots in long-established folk traditions.

Hairstyles and furnishings are shown in great detail – on the left a group of musicians play clearly identifiable instruments

This roundel decorated a crossbar on the stupa railing – it shows a scene of courtly life, illustrating a story of a former incarnation of the Buddha

THE PROBLEMS OF DATING
Dating rock art poses a problem. One clue is similarities in style between rock art and artwork known from dateable domestic contexts. Another is the depiction of artefacts whose date is known – such as the Bronze Age tools and weapons in this Swedish rock painting. The different kinds of boat illustrated give valuable information on sea-faring. Other contemporary Bronze Age rock art in Europe shows aspects of agriculture, such as ploughing with oxen.

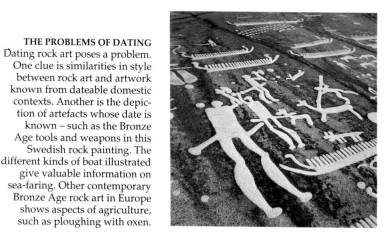

Elephant, wheel, and horse are symbols that allow us to identify the main figure here as the Chakravartin – the Universal Monarch

Buddha's
renunciation of
his princely life

Tiered umbrellas on
the summit of stupas
symbolize royalty

Birth of the
Buddha

Queen Maya's
dream of Buddha's
conception

A COBBLER'S TALE
Even though art is often
symbolic or has a deeper meaning,
it can give excellent detailed
information about the daily life of its
creators. Greek painted pottery often
depicts mythological subjects, but
they also show us many aspects of
Greek life. Here a cobbler is cutting
and shaping strips of leather –
above him hang finished sandals,
boots, and the tools of his trade. By
closely examining stylistic details,
scholars have been able to identify
the work of individual painters.
Some even signed their artwork.

Some stupa carvings
show many decorative
elements on the upper
portion of the dome

Other carvings depict
lavish flower garlands

Surviving slabs from otherwise completely destroyed
stupa depict similar stupas,
giving us a clear picture
of its original appearance

Seated lions guard
the gateway

Worshippers
surround
the stupa

Viking warrior
burials contained
weapons but no
armour, so
artwork like this
provides valuable
information

The stupa was
surrounded by a
stone railing, its
outer face decorated
with lotus roundels

Buddha with
worshippers

THE WALRUS AND ITS IVORY
The walrus ivory chessmen from Scotland's Isle of Lewis
depict Viking society. The pawns are foot soldiers, while
the knights, bishops, kings, and queens represent the
upper classes in the social hierarchy. This knight shows
his expensive warrior equipment – horse and trappings,
including stirrups, which were a recent innovation.

Walking among the past

MUCH OF A TOWN'S PAST can be discovered just by looking at it carefully, for how the original settlement was laid out governs subsequent construction. When old buildings are torn down, the shape of the space remaining can be traced in the layout of the new constructions. Curved streets may mark where there once was a town wall, now long vanished. The architectural styles of houses and the organization of streets differ greatly throughout the ages. These may now survive, but in a modified form – old houses divided into flats, tiny cottages knocked into one. Looking more closely, architectural details can reveal individual structures' history, while place names can tell of vanished features or changed purposes.

SECOND THOUGHTS
Cordoba's mosque was extended in A.D. 987, its earlier outer wall becoming part of the interior. Such alterations to a building's fabric are valuable clues for reconstructing its history.

THE MIHRAB
This new mihrab (sacred niche) was built when Cordoba's mosque was extended in A.D. 961. Although clearly related in design to earlier parts, this and other elements of the extension are more imaginative and their decoration much richer.

Mihrab was the mosque's focal point of worship

Typical Arab feature

Horseshoe arch, typical of southern Spain, is derived from Visigothic architecture

CHRISTIAN VANDALISM
In 1236, Cordoba was reconquered by the Christian rulers of Spain and the mosque was altered to become a church. But in the 1500s, the entire centre was destroyed to build an ornate cathedral. The gaudy decoration of its dome contrasts with the Moslem mihrab's restrained beauty.

THE DOOR TO MAGNIFICENCE
The Visigoths seized Cordoba from the Romans, but later lost it to the Arabs. Little survives from the Visigothic period (c. A.D. 500–719), but their church was the basis for the mosque built here in A.D 786. St Stephen's Gate, the oldest remaining entrance to the mosque, was built into surviving walls.

Roman pillar survived to become part of the later structure

ROME STANDS FOREVER
Several major modern streets of the Roman town of Cordoba, with Roman milestones, still follow the Roman layout. Portions of the wall still stand, showing the town's original extent. Many pillars show where impressive Roman buildings once stood (left).

ON HIGH
Cordoba's cathedral dominates the mosque. Around it, narrow streets preserve a portion of the medieval city – its Jewish quarter (Juderia), whose name records its former inhabitants. Bounding this is part of the Roman city wall, a legible historical document showing its original construction Arab additions, Reconquest damage, and later rebuilding.

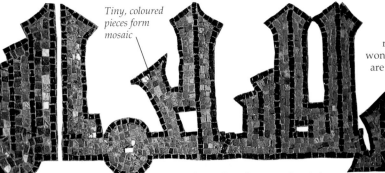

Calligraphy and flowers decorate Moslem architecture – showing people and animals is prohibited by Islamic religion

Tiny, coloured pieces form mosaic

INSIDE THE MOSQUE
The construction of the great mosque at Cordoba reused Roman and Visigothic pillars from an earlier church, but significantly altered both its layout and its structure. By the addition of stone pillars and arches above the earlier columns, the original restricted church was transformed into a tall, light, spacious structure.

Horseshoe arches echo mosque's exterior, with alternating brick and stone

Truncated pyramid added above column supports massive stone pillar

Details show how Roman and Visigothic column capitals differ

Extensions to the mosque can be identified from such details as variations in the style of arch used

Roman and Visigothic columns and capitals were reused

Why excavate?

Black-glazed drinking vessel from the François tomb, 4th century B.C.

A LEISURELY INTEREST
Demands for artefacts created a tomb-robbing industry, which still continues. Etruscan tombs, with their fine frescoes and reliefs, were an interesting curiosity for gentle-folk on the Grand Tour in the 1700s.

FROM THE 14TH-CENTURY ONWARDS, collectors have sought many superb artefacts of antiquity. Later excavators tried to find out more about the past which they knew only from ancient texts. In the 1800s great lost civilizations, as well as unknown prehistoric cultures, were discovered. Geological advances demonstrated the great anti-quity of the world and its inhabitants. An ordered picture of the past emerged, but dating was a problem. Excavators collected material to build chronological sequences. Now modern excavators, freed by scientific dating from this need, can investigate all aspects of life. The extensive treasure hunting of the past now has no justification.

UNCOVERING THE TRUTH?
The François tomb at Vulci, Italy contained many wonderful artefacts, such as this drinking vessel. A fresco in the tomb showed a well-known episode from Roman history, but it illustrated a quite different Etruscan version, thereby casting doubts on the Roman account. An important conclusion was drawn – that archaeology could contribute to knowledge in its own right, rather than merely illustrating history.

Mirror, 300–200 B.C., is inscribed "Grave gift of Suthina"

Seianti Thanunia Tlesnasa of ancient Clusium, shown lying on the lid of her sarcophagus and holding a mirror

VANDALISM ON A LARGE SCALE
The 19th century saw the rediscovery of great civilizations. Spectacular architecture and sculpture (palaces, tombs, and temples) attracted most attention, but national pride played a shameful role in excavation. Here at Nineveh in Iraq, French and British teams competed to carry off monumental remains to adorn their own national museums.

REFLECTIONS OF ANTIQUITY
Bronze mirrors were among the most beautiful of Etruscan objects, often intricately engraved. In the late 1800s, catalogues, such as one devoted to Etruscan mirrors, helped scholars reconstruct the history of the shadowy Etruscans.

ETRUSCAN PLACES
Excavation methods in the mid-1800s were still in their infancy. Though systematic recording of finds was growing, the emphasis was still on retrieving objects from prominent sites, such as these Etruscan tombs at Orvieto in central Italy. Etruscan remains provided a patriotic ancestry for the newly unified Italian nation.

Gold wreath
of ivy leaves,
c. 300–200 B.C.

Exquisite
gold earrings,
c. 350–300 B.C.

ALL THAT GLITTERS
At first excavators collected beautiful and valuable objects for their own sake, but later they sought artefacts that were distinctive and would contribute to our knowledge of the past. Modern excavators actively seek the more mundane artefacts their predecessors threw away, for they can tell us as much if not more about how life was lived in the past.

GREECE IN ITALY
In the early 1900s, many archaeologists believed that European culture developed from the civilizations of Western Asia and Greece. Etruscans, whose frescos depicted Greek legends, were thought to come from eastern Greece. More recent excavations demonstrated Etruscan culture developed locally, but that trade made Greek things fashionable.

RESTING IN PEACE
Excavations of the 1800s concentrated on tombs, yielding fine pottery and sarcophagi. Recognizing changes in style of artefacts became an archaeological preoccupation. This painted sarcophagus, dating from 300-150 B.C., is well within the Roman period but still copies the Etruscan style.

Useful mortar unearthed by excavation of Etruscan settlement

EXCAVATION NOW
Preoccupation with the great and glorious continued well into the 20th century. But today excavation is done both to save the past from destruction and to answer particular questions. Field investigations followed by site excavations answer questions about the daily lives, industry, religion, and politics of the Etruscans.

Digging up the past

ARCHAEOLOGISTS excavate "sites". This elastic term ranges from a hide for hunting to a complete town. During excavation a site is carefully taken apart in the reverse order to how it was formed. The topsoil is removed first to reveal "features", which refer to anomalies created by people like pits or postholes, walls, roads, or yards. Archaeologists then look also for "layers", distinct deposits of soil which show differences in the way they were formed, due to environmental factors or human activities. One of an archaeologist's chief skills must be the ability to detect variations in soil, such as colour, texture, and feel.

Dental picks for fine work and fragile remains

Photo scale used when photographing small features or objects

Small brush to clean away grains of loose soil around objects

10-m cloth tape for general site recording – laying out the site, planning, and section drawing

Plumb bob for correct vertical plotting

LAYING OUT THE SITE
At the start of an excavation, a fixed point is established, of known height above or below sea level. This is the point to which the height of all measurements on site will be related. A fixed base line is set up and its position mapped. All subsequent horizontal points, including the trenches to be excavated, are worked out in relation to this. During excavation surveying equipment records the heights of different layers and finds.

TOOLS FOR THE JOB
After removal of vegetation and topsoil, the area is cleared to reveal the uppermost archaeological features. These are investigated individually, using small picks or trowels. Loose soil is removed with a hand shovel and trowel or brush, but delicate objects may require dental picks, teaspoons, and tiny brushes. Recording is absolutely vital, so archaeologists also have measuring and drawing equipment. Wheelbarrows and buckets remove soil to the spoil heap – and provide seats at tea breaks!

ENTRENCHED VIEW
Before an excavation begins, the site director must decide where to start digging, then plan and recruit the people needed to carry out the work – experienced supervisors, specialists, and diggers (often students or local labourers). Permission for the excavation to start must be obtained as well as funding for the cost of excavation. Once everything is ready, the parts of the site to be excavated are marked out, often in squares or rectangles. Shown above is a model of the site of Tell es-Sa'idiyeh in Jordan at the end of the 1993 season.

LIFE'S UPS AND DOWNS
Remains of the past are found at three levels – structures sticking up, ground level, and holes going down. So when a site is excavated, archaeologists will first encounter remains of walls sticking up into the topsoil. From these, excavators can make a plan of contemporary structures which are then individually excavated down to their ground level, followed by their pits and other holes below ground. In this step-by-step manner, the site is taken apart, from present to past.

SOGGY SLOGGING
This brushwood trackway in England's Somerset Levels contrasts strongly with the excavation in Jordan. This wetland site means soggy digging conditions and waterlogged finds. A plastic shelter keeps rain off diggers but, more importantly, prevents sun drying out the waterlogged road. The peat is peeled away with ice lolly sticks and plastic spatulas. Toe boards lessen pressure on wood below the surface. Despite differences, all excavations share the same basic principles, aims, and hard work!

Bricklayer's pointing trowel, the all-purpose tool

Handpick, the most widely used digging tool in the Near East

Position of every object and bone is planned

A GRAVE SITUATION
Usually burials are in a grave, cut from the surface of a particular period. Inside this may be a coffin or a jar, containing a skeleton (left), with its grave goods. The bronze javelin showed this burial at Tell es-Sa'idiyeh was of a warrior – its corrosion has preserved mineralized traces of linen, indicating that the person had been tightly bound.

CARE OF THE DEAD
Excavating a burial is a delicate operation involving fine dental tools, brushes and trowels. Grave goods can be tiny, such as minute beads, so great care is exercised. Often all soil from the grave pit is finely sieved to recover any tiny item that has been missed.

Label identifies individual layer in the section

COMMITTED TO PAPER
Detailed recording is an absolutely vital part of excavation. As well as photographs and written records, detailed drawings are made of all features and deposits. Plans record the horizontal aspects of the site, such as arrangements of house walls or details of grave pits and their contents. Section drawings record the vertical aspects such as the profile and fills of features like pits. Everything on an excavation drawing is carefully and accurately recorded to scale.

These jars were found with others in a complex that was probably an administrative centre for the distribution of locally-made olive oil

SIGNIFICANT OTHERS
Excavated finds are divided into two categories – small finds, and the rest. Small finds are objects of individual significance, such as grave goods. What is a small find depends on what material a site yields. Each is given an individual number and its horizontal and vertical position is precisely recorded. Other things are just finds, and are collected and recorded only by context. The distinction continues with the processing of the finds – small finds are carefully cleaned, perhaps by professional conservators, while other finds are often vigorously cleaned with water and scrubbing brushes.

Two large storage jars from Jordan's Tell es-Sa'idiyeh – these were probably used for storing olive oil, a major export from the area

Things in their place

WHAT DID PEOPLE DO IN THE PAST and why? Artefacts only provide information about how they were made, their makers' artistic abilities, and perhaps how they were used. Bones alone have little meaning. Features such as buildings tell us how they were constructed, and deposits inside, above, or below these features tell us how soil accumulated. But put all this information together and there is almost unlimited data. Context (where things come from and how they relate to each other) is one of the most important aspects of archaeological investigation, which explains why archaeologists are so enraged by looting. This takes objects out of their context, destroying any information they could give.

WHAT'S GOING ON?
Finds give clues to activities once carried out in individual rooms of excavated buildings. Deposits which accumulated later contain evidence of subsequent activity there.

Wall of mud-brick structure

Jars placed against wall

Site notebook shows where objects are sited within a structure – all are carefully labelled

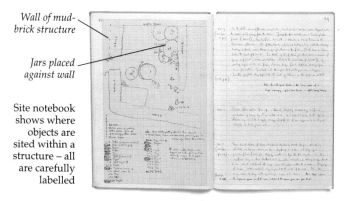

CAPTURED CONTEXT
Many objects are left in their original place within abandoned buildings. Where they were found and what they are may provide information about the building's function. Making detailed plans of these structures and objects in their place is an important part of site recording.

PATTERNS OF ACTIVITY
Remains found together may show a single activity performed in the past. Relationships between structures within a settlement show how it was organized socially and economically (above). For example, by refitting the pieces knapped (struck) from a piece of flint, the stages in a flint tool's manufacture can be reconstructed. Useless discarded animal bones associated with flint tools may show a butchery site, while meat-bearing bones from the same animal show where people ate.

PACKAGED INFORMATION
Chance plays a part in what accumulates through time in ordinary contexts because of loss or abandonment. Burials are very special because they contain material deliberately deposited at one time in the past, an association which had meaning for the people who made the burial. This means that quite detailed conclusions about society can be drawn from burials.

Crouched position of burials within single or double jars may symbolize a return to the mother's womb

Double jar burial from Tell es-Sa'idiyeh in Jordan

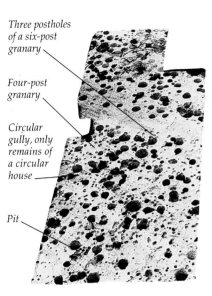

Three postholes of a six-post granary

Four-post granary

Circular gully, only remains of a circular house

Pit

Part of Danebury hillfort, showing a variety of pits and postholes

A JOIN-THE-DOTS PUZZLE
Super-imposed ground surfaces show a site's sequence. How can we understand sites, such as England's Danebury hillfort, where the ancient surface has disappeared? Lived in for over 500 years, Danebury has 4,500 storage pits, 18,000 post-holes, and thousands of stake-holes! Fortunately it has a key – remnants of stratified deposits with a pottery sequence, roundhouses, and square or rectangular gran-aries. Using this knowledge, individual holes were dated by the pottery in them, and plans of typical structures were identified.

Pompeii's residents hid in cellars, hoping to escape the blast, but died from poisonous gases

NO ESCAPE!
In the 1800s, visitors to Italy's Herculaneum and Pompeii saw for themselves the results of Vesuvius' eruption in 79 A.D. These sights inspired them to create dramatic works of art and literature depicting lives that had ended so suddenly, such as this artist's impression of the scene in the wine cellars of a villa at Pompeii (above) where 17 people died in the poses depicted.

Ordinary possessions such as pots were left behind when people fled – these now give invaluable information about everyday life

CAUGHT IN THE ACT
Most things which archae-ologists find were lost, abandoned, or thrown away – such as hairpins or coins dropped acciden-tally, discarded rubbish, things too worn, too trivial, or too large to be taken when people moved house. These items reveal a great deal, but the picture is incomplete. Although burials, hoards, and ritual offerings are deliberately deposited, they only tell us about certain aspects of life. But sudden disasters, such as the asphyxiation of Herculaneum's inhabi-tants (left) by hot ash and gas, are exceptionally informative because they "freeze" existence, allowing us to reconstruct people's whole way of life at that moment.

Vegetation will eventually destroy this site at Herculaneum

Mounds and monuments

MOUNDS ARE ARTIFICIAL HILLS designed to dominate the landscape. These and other monuments, built to impress and to attract attention, make a public statement – this is our land or our king is the greatest, and so on. The way monuments are distributed across the landscape gives important clues to the organization of past societies, as do the burials they may contain. A mound burial may underline a ruler's importance, while lesser mortals lie in flat graves. On the other hand a mound or monument, like the European megaliths, may cover jumbled skeletal remains of many individuals – an "equal-access" tomb for a more democratic society.

HEAPS OF POWER
Looking at patterns of burial practices provides helpful clues to past social organization. In this map of 1610, the massive burial mounds at England's Sutton Hoo are clearly visible. Recent excavations have also revealed many flat graves in the area. It appears to be a cemetery with different social ranks and the grave goods support this.

WORTH HIS WEIGHT IN GOLD
The richness of their grave goods may reflect the status of different individuals. But what was considered valuable in the past? Archaeologists think that rare, hard to obtain, or far-travelled materials, or objects that required time or special skill to make, had special value. Sutton Hoo's grave goods, like this gold buckle, were clearly very valuable.

Intricate decoration of interlaced birds and animals

ROW, ROW, ROW THE BOAT
Gold and jewelled belt fittings included the remains of a purse. This contained gold coins, interpreted as payment for the steersman and 40 oarsmen. The most recent coin gives a date not earlier than A.D. 625 for the burial.

Bronze foil panels decorate the iron helmet

GHOST SHIP
Meticulous excavations of mounds at Sutton Hoo in the late 1930s revealed Anglo-Saxon remains including a small boat. In the largest mound was a massive ship. All that survived of this 27-m (90-ft) long ship were a hard crust in the sand (the "ghost" of the decayed timbers) and the iron rivets fastening the timbers together. Poorly preserved grave goods, of unprecedented splendour, survived inside a decayed wooden central chamber.

A TOAST TO DEATH
Due to acid soil, the Sutton Hoo metal objects were fragmentary and poorly preserved, while bone, horn, textiles, and wood had almost completely vanished. Painstaking recording of the position of every fragment enabled objects to be pieced together and reconstructed.

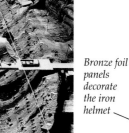

Drinking horn made from a small aurochs

Reconstructed part

Original fragment of silver-gilt decoration

Iron crest had gilded bronze animal heads with garnet eyes

Helmet belonged to King Raedwald, overlord of the English kings, who died in A.D. 625

MYSTERIOUS MONUMENTS

Not all mounds contain burials and not all monuments are mounds. Temples or cathedrals are clearly for religious observances. Other monuments, like these massive ranks of stones dominating the landscape at Carnac in France, are much more enigmatic. Their purpose, hidden now, was obviously very important to their builders. Estimates of the vast amounts of labour involved give some idea of the size of the work force mobilized by their creators.

WARRIOR KING

Archaeologists believe that grave goods are chosen to reflect the roles the deceased played in society. So what do the grave goods of Sutton Hoo tell us? Their richness shows their owner's great importance, borne out by the labour expended in his ship burial and mound. This helmet (left) and weaponry indicate that he was a warrior, a necessity for a leader in warlike Anglo-Saxon society. Objects thought to be a sceptre and royal standard suggest their owner was a king.

Reconstruction of helmet in 1949

Gilded bronze mouth, nose, and eyebrows formed bird with outstretched wings and gnashing teeth

Hinged neck and ear guards, attached to cap forged from single piece of iron

WRONGLY ASSEMBLED

The helmet was found in about 500 small fragments, but only the gilded parts had survived in any recognizable form. Recent doubts about how accurate the first reconstruction was (above), prompted a complete dismantling and a new attempt. It was a painstaking task – putting together a jigsaw of which most pieces were missing and many surviving ones broken – but a triumph for conservation.

Hot and dry

Creature embroidered into fabric

PERFECTLY PRESERVED
The dry coastal regions of Peru have yielded many desiccated human burials, complete with food, basketry, and beautiful textiles.

ORGANIC REMAINS come from such extreme environments as bogs, polar, or desert regions, since micro-organisms that cause their decay need temperatures above freezing, moisture, and air. Deserts are not easily inhabited by humans, so most of their archaeological treasures have come from places where local water supplies have been used for irrigation agriculture. Carbonization (burning without oxygen) removes moisture from materials, such as carbonized grain, ensuring their survival. More spectacular but rare is preservation by volcanic eruptions, which destroyed life but preserved death.

A BLAST FROM THE PAST
On 24 August, A.D. 79, Vesuvius erupted, covering the towns of Pompeii in ash and Herculaneum in volcanic mud. Thousands of people were asphyxiated, and their bodies rapidly covered in ash and pumice, which cooled to form a solid rock case. Inside these cases, bodies decayed leaving a mould of their shapes. Pompeii's first serious excavator, Giuseppe Fiorelli, developed a technique of producing plaster casts of these body moulds in the 1860s.

Baker's stamp still visible on loaf

Some marks of clothing, pressed tightly against his body by ash and pumice, still visible

BURNT BREAD
Pompeii's streets survive frozen in time, complete with houses, gardens, and shops. Among these are several bakeries, with counters at the front and massive lava milling stones in the back, along with bread ovens from which completely carbonized round loaves have been recovered.

Cast of individual sitting out his last moments of life

Grass brush from Central Asia, 7th–8th century A.D.

THE SANDS OF TIME
Centuries ago many prosperous towns, dependent on canal irrigation for agriculture, were established in the inhospitable deserts of Central Asia along the Silk Route from China to the West. Following detailed information in ancient records, Sir Aurel Stein endured great hardship to trace these settlements in the early 1900s.

WOODEN CAPITAL
Stein uncovered many ancient settlements, their wooden architecture undecayed, but eroded by fierce winds. The most important buildings had beautifully carved wood and stucco decoration, like this 3rd-century A.D. carved capital. Official records show an interesting cultural blend: typical Chinese wooden tablets but written in an Indian script and language, with Western-style seals.

Roman meals usually began with eggs and ended with fruit

CRACKED EGGS
Many private houses at Pompeii and Herculaneum still contained domestic objects in their place – wooden furniture such as a table and a cot, and wooden cupboards with pottery and glass vessels. Some shops had wooden racks supporting amphorae full of charred grain and other scorched food. Tables were laid with dishes of fruit, nuts, and eggs (above).

HOUSEHOLD GOODS
The houses of ordinary people in Stein's Central Asian sites contained such well-preserved domestic artefacts as grass brooms, wooden chopsticks, felt textiles, and even mousetraps. Recovering objects from rubbish pits, Stein complained that the smell from these had also survived the centuries! His most exciting discoveries were from caves near Tun-Huang in China, where he found wonderful Buddhist paintings on silk (pp. 50–51) and a vast library of manuscripts in many different languages and scripts.

Cliff Palace pueblo at Mesa Verde, Colorado, USA

VANISHED IN A PUFF OF SMOKE
Dry sites from the New World have preserved rope sandals, while hobnails in Roman burials show their boots were once there. These leather shoes, minus their owners, survive in a carbonized state at Pompeii.

Carbonized soles of shoes from Pompeii

LIFE AT THE TOP
The hot, dry regions in the American southwest have preserved many organic materials, such as plant remains and coprolites (preserved faeces). Pueblo settlements were constructed on the plains and later on sides of cliffs for better defence (above). In the 1920s, A.E. Douglass pioneered the technique of dendrochronology (pp. 54–55) on wood preserved in these pueblos. This permits wood used in the construction of individual rooms to be precisely dated, thereby establishing the building history of the pueblos.

Preserved by ice

THE COLDEST REGIONS ON EARTH, such as Alaska, Siberia, Greenland, and the Alps, can act as a deep freeze, preserving burials, accident victims, and their possessions, and anything else buried in the frozen ground. The soft tissue of well-preserved bodies gives valuable information such as what diseases they died from and what they ate. Analysis shows Eskimos often have black lungs from breathing in oil lamp smoke and lived mainly on marine foods like fish and seals. High cholesterol levels from a blubber-rich diet caused heart disease. Ice has also preserved wood, textiles, food, and garments – Eskimo parkas, boots, and trousers, and a wonderful array of organic finds from the chiefs' barrows of Pazyryk in Siberia.

Chain stitch embroidery on silk saddlecloth of a pheasant or phoenix

FLOWN FAR FROM HOME
The Pazyryk saddles were made of two joined leather cushions stuffed with deer hair, with wooden bows front and back and a felt cover, usually decorated with cut-out felt designs. One cover is a priceless Chinese silk, such as were made for the marriage of a princess.

Leather ear and horn were detachable

Twisted posture of animal – typical of Pazyryk's artistic style

This side of a leather flask from Barrow 1 has a mosaic pattern of white and blue fur shapes

Pieces of leopard skin make up the reverse side

RAMMED INTO POSITION
At Pazyryk in Siberia, barrows were erected to cover the wooden burial chambers of chiefs and their women c. 400 B.C. Dug in summer when the ground was soft, the underground, log-built chambers froze in their first winter and never thawed again – until they were excavated in the 1940s, using boiling water. Dendrochronology (pp. 54–55) on the logs showed the five excavated barrows were built over 48 years. These barrows had preserved a rich array of grave goods in various organic materials.

IN THE BAG
The Pazyryk graves yielded many fur and leather containers, similar to those used by modern nomadic tribes. One flask in Barrow 2 had contained cheese, while others still had plant remains in them, including narcotic hemp seeds and imported coriander. Small earthenware bottles had once contained koumiss (fermented mare's milk). Such details show that the lives of the people of Pazyryk were similar to those of their horse-keeping neighbours, the Scythians, described by Classical authors.

Horn frontal plate from saddle of one of seven sacrificed horses in Barrow 2

RIDING INTO THE SUNSET

The people of Pazyryk were horse-riding herders, keeping cattle, sheep, goats, and especially horses, which they raised for meat, milk, and skins and traded with the settled peoples of Western Asia and China. The chiefs buried here were accompanied by their sacrificed riding horses. The horse trappings included saddles, leather bridles decorated with wooden or horn carvings, and horses' face masks bearing elaborate headdresses.

Horned tiger

Gorytus (bow case and quiver)

Stylized goose

Felt wall hanging shows typical horse and archery equipment

DRESSED TO KILL

The Pazyryk barrows are rich in art. Felt cut-out designs portray carnivorous beasts attacking animals. Wooden carvings show men with thick beards. The felt wall hanging from Barrow 5 has riders sporting fine moustaches. The buried chiefs themselves were clean shaven, but one had an artificial beard made of human hair on a leather strip.

Small carnivore

Deer shaped monster with elaborate antlers

Tattoos on right arm display predators and their victims, some half mythological

SCARRED FOR LIFE

The burials at Pazyryk did not freeze immediately, so although textiles and wooden objects survived intact, the flesh of sacrificed horses had time to decay, leaving only their skeletons. The human bodies were better preserved as they had been embalmed. The body of a chief from Barrow 2 bore the remains of elaborate tattoos. The tattoos had probably been made by pricking the design deeply into the skin and rubbing soot into it, which gave a bluish tinge in life.

Marine archaeology

THE SEA HAS YIELDED some extraordinarily well-preserved remains of wrecked ships and drowned settlements, but it is not a gentle preserver. Undersea remains are attacked by salt, marine organisms, and currents. But once the remains settle into the seabed and are covered with silts, their physical destruction virtually ceases. Locating wrecks, like England's *Mary Rose*, is made very difficult by the seabed's shifting silts, but sonar devices can assist reconnaissance. Underwater excavation, recording, and photography are hampered by poor visibility, though the ability to approach remains from any angle allows three-dimensional video recording, impossible on land. Physical excavation is easier underwater, but excavators are restricted by the time they can safely work there.

LIFTING THE *MARY ROSE*
Submerged in the seabed for centuries, the *Mary Rose's* starboard side survived virtually intact. Excavated between 1966 and 1982, the contents of the hull were carefully recorded and removed. The fragile hull was lifted, using a special tubular steel frame, into a steel cradle lined with airbags. On 11 October 1982, the *Mary Rose* was brought to the surface.

First the hull was lifted onto the cradle underwater, providing support for raising it above water

THE PRIDE OF THE FLEET
The *Mary Rose* (inaccurately but attractively depicted above), was built for England's Henry VIII in 1509–1510. One of the most advanced vessels of her time, she sank during a battle with a French invasion fleet in 1545.

LIFE ON THE *MARY ROSE*
This model shows the surviving portion of the *Mary Rose's* hull. The galley in her hold held a large firebox and four copper cauldrons. On the deck above, neatly stacked plates and bowls were found. Around the companionway leading out of the hold the injured or sick were laid. Better medical provision was provided on the main deck where the barber-surgeon's cabin was located. Many bones of the *Mary Rose's* crew and soldiers were found, some trying to escape. The ship went down so fast that many died where they stood.

Model of the *Mary Rose's* hull, as she lay on the seabed

Flint ballast in hold kept ship well down in the water

Stored logs used for galley fuel, cables, and barrels of tar

Steel support cradle

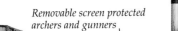

Removable screen protected archers and gunners

THE *MARY ROSE* RECONSTRUCTED
The recovery of well-preserved wrecks like the *Mary Rose* provides us with a wealth of detail about the shipbuilding technology and design of their time, information not available from often inaccurate contemporary illustrations. The hull of the *Mary Rose* was carvel built. Her guns on the main gundeck were fired through gunports with wooden gunport lids, while on the weather deck, visible here, wooden blinds which protected the men against enemy fire or heavy seas could be removed to run out the guns.

Model of the Mary Rose, viewed from the port side (above)

Main deck gunport

Swivel gun

Hatch

Upper deck gunport

Bonaventure mast

Bowcastle gun

Mizzen mast

Bronze gun in front of sterncastle

Model of the Mary Rose viewed from above

UNDER THE SEA
Seabed silts can often be easily excavated using hands or brushes and the spoil (waste soil) removed using airlifts. But these silts are also easily stirred up by currents or the divers themselves, exacerbating the problem of already poor visibility.

Castle deck – the highest deck in the ship

Barber-surgeon's cabin contained his chest of medicines and shaving equipment

Ointments and field-dressings were among the barber-surgeon's equipment, also a wooden mallet used with an amputation knife

CONSTANT CONSERVATION
The cradle in which the *Mary Rose* was lifted still supports her in the dry dock where, in order to preserve the wood, she is sprayed with chilled water for at least 20 hours each day. Regular tests ensure that physical and biological decay does not occur.

Main deck held guns as well as carpenter and barber-surgeon's cabins – where many men were trapped when the ship sank

Orlop deck for stowing stores, equipment, food, hand weapons, and personal possessions

Oak hull is carvel-built (smooth, edge-to-edge planking)

Stern post

Elm keel

Galley

Continued on next page

Conserving and treating

Some organic materials like leather and wood can be preserved under the sea, while others like horn and linen are destroyed by marine micro-organisms. Much of the *Mary Rose*'s iron has corroded away, leaving only stains to show what was once there. What survived had to be stabilized to prevent further deterioration. Where appropriate, objects were carefully cleaned with brushes, soluble salts washed out, and insoluble iron corrosion products removed using chemicals.

Inscription on both sides of turned beech wood bowl

WOODEN BOWL
Although wooden objects preserved under water retain their original appearance, the internal structure of the wood has broken down. To preserve them, the water must be replaced with PEG (polyethylene glycol), a type of wax. First soluble salts are removed by washing and insoluble salts by soaking in a chemical solution. The object is soaked in a series of increasingly strong PEG solutions to replace the water in it with PEG. Then it is freeze-dried and stored in a humid environment.

Slashed decoration on high-vamped leather shoe

LEATHER SHOE
Various leather objects were recovered from the *Mary Rose*, including shoes – some still on skeletons' feet. Clothing included woollen stockings, caps, and sleeves. Satin, silk, and lace trimmings survived.

Inscription of Henry VIII

Emblem of the Tudor Rose

Bronze muzzle-loading gun weighs 1135 kg (2500 lb)

Reproduction wheeled carriage built of elm with wrought iron fastenings

CANNON CONSERVATON
Encrustations on the *Mary Rose*'s wrought and cast iron cannon were chipped away before the guns were stabilized by heating them in a hydrogen reduction furnace. This turned the oxidized iron back into metallic iron. Bronze objects were cleaned of harmful chemicals by repeated washing.

SURE SHOT
All the *Mary Rose*'s guns were found loaded and ready to fire. Various types of ammunition were used by her gunners, including massive stone cannon balls, lead and cast iron shot. Two-piece moulds for casting small lead shot were found at the stern of the ship.

Large stone shot weighing 10 kg (22 lb)

Stone shot weighing 4.5 kg (10 lb)

Iron shot weighing 6 kg (14 lb)

Medium stone shot

Iron-lead shot

Hinged lid

Horn reinforcements on the bows have disintegrated

FRAGILE FLAGON
Pewter must be treated to remove marine encrustations and harmful chemicals, although some objects, like this flagon, are too fragile and must be stabilized as found. Pewter vessels belonged to the *Mary Rose*'s officers, while the soldiers and crew used wooden plates and drinking vessels (tiggs). Also found aboard were meat, vegetables, fruit, herbs, and spices. Wooden and pottery jars in the barber-surgeon's chest contained ointments and medicines.

Encrustation of pewter caused by action of barnacles and other micro-organisms underwater

Bubbles show that pewter flagon has been conserved, but it can never be restored to its former silvery sheen without risk of object disintegrating

WOODEN BOWS
Despite the importance of the English longbow, no surviving examples were known until the discoveries from the *Mary Rose*. Some archery equipment was still stored in chests, while other longbows were found with the archers at action stations, ready to defend the ship. Other surviving archery equipment included leather wristguards and 24-hole leather discs in which arrows were stored.

Pewter flagon – over 70 pieces of pewter were recovered from the Mary Rose

Yew bows skilfully cut to provide both strength and flexibility

Sturdy base to avoid movement when ship was sailing

Freshwater preservation

WETLAND SITES such as peatbogs and fens are an archaeologist's dream. Artefacts from past daily lives have been very well preserved, because the oxygen needed by bacteria which cause organic remains to decay is absent. Wood, leather, and other organic materials from wetland sites give us a much more complete picture than dry sites, while plant, snail, and insect remains provide valuable information on local environments. However, acid peat bogs destroy materials like pottery and calcium in bones which survive on dry land sites. Although valuable, wetland sites present problems. During excavation, fragile, waterlogged remains must be kept wet and excavators must be very careful not to crush them.

Grass roots (living layer of peat)

Pieces of wood denote remains of ancient structures

Plant fibre – such organic material allows the sequence of the peat development to be radiocarbon dated

Head shows he had been hit with blunt instrument, strangled, and throat cut

Slot in closely fitting wooden box for a sharpening stone, but it was not found

Fingernails show that, like many bog bodies, he had not done rough manual work

WET AND DAMP
Peat slowly forms from vegetation in water-logged areas, over thousands of years. Commercial exploitation and land drainage is rapidly destroying it, along with the evidence it contains. Examination of the sides of drainage ditches in England's East Anglian fens led to the discovery of Flag Fen, a remarkable artificial island from the Late Bronze Age.

BOGMAN
Peatbogs from Northern Europe have yielded startling finds of well-preserved bodies. Most (probably religious sacrifices) belong to the Iron Age. England's Lindow Man is typical – he had been executed and laid naked in a boggy pool. Scientific investigation can reveal much about bog bodies – Lindow Man's "0" blood group and charred bread in his gut.

Leaf shape was typical of Late Bronze Age swords

Bronze stopper

Bead

Fibula (like modern safety pin)

Swan's neck pin

Miniature tin wheel

Bronze plate brooch

Bronze stick pin

TREASURED TOOLS
This pair of bronze shears in a wooden box from Flag Fen was a unique find. Previously, such shears were known only in iron. Probably of Iron Age date, they could have been used for shearing sheep and for cutting anything from willow wands to hair. Lindow Man's moustache had been trimmed with shears shortly before his death.

JEWELLED ASSORTMENT
These spectacular Iron Age ornaments, all imperfect or deliberately damaged, were among the discoveries from Flag Fen island and post alignment. Many were locally made, but the unusual wheel was probably from Switzerland. Pins and brooches were used for fastening clothing.

Verdegris – green patina formed on bronze surface after exposure to water-logged peat over a long period of time

Well-defined midrib

Socket for wooden handle

Swords like this were made in Europe in the Bronze Age, around 1800 B.C.

Spearhead – an uncommon offering at Flag Fen

Break in this sword was done deliberately before it was thrown into the water

OFFERINGS TO THE GODS

A 1-km (0.6-mi) line of posts, perhaps a territorial boundary, led from dry land out to the artificial island of Flag Fen. Masses of Late Bronze Age and Iron Age objects, particularly swords and pins, as well as animal and some human bones, were deposited all along the inshore side of the post alignment. Depositing fine expensive objects in watery places may have been a religious practice in Iron Age Europe.

Late Bronze Age (c. 1000 B.C.) swords were among the most common offerings at Flag Fen

WOODEN BARRIER

Any wooden structure from the prehistoric period is a rare find – and a nightmare to excavate. Much of the work carried out at Flag Fen has been done uncomfortably suspended above the wooden posts on horizontal scaffolding. The five rows of oak posts formed a 1-km (0.6 mi) long barrier. Its floor was covered in wood chippings and white sand.

Distinctive shape is useful for dating by typology

Split oak plank – before invention of saws, timbers were split using wooden wedges

Slot through which plank was pegged to ground

In oak timbers such as these, dendrochronology is used to work out building sequence at Flag Fen

Sharpened end for driving timber directly into ground – sometimes marks of axe used for shaping the wood are visible

Upright posts stood over 2 m (6 ft) high

TIMBERS FROM FLAG FEN

The principal timbers at Flag Fen were oak and alder with some ash. Some of the oak was used as roundwood, but most had been split into planks. Horizontal timbers were carefully fixed in place by pegs, which were made of coppiced wood, so indicating local woodland management (pp. 46–47). Details in the five rows of posts show the expertise of Bronze Age carpentry.

Conservation of materials

MANY REMAINS OF THE PAST have survived well – until they are discovered and exposed to modern conditions. Often excavated materials must be treated to stabilize them and so prevent any deterioration. An exception is material to be dated or scientifically analyzed – this must be delivered to the laboratory as found. For example, waterlogged wood must be kept wet, while iron, such as the *Mary Rose*'s cannons, may be heated to stabilize the metal. Objects must be cleaned, either mechanically or chemically. Often this is done on site, although delicate remains are cleaned in the laboratory. Once conserved, objects are ready for study or display.

Pottery sherds emerging from the soil of the Jordanian site of Tell es-Sa'idiyeh (pp. 22–23)

Glue is applied in an extremely thin layer

The matching sherds, one edge glued, are carefully aligned so they fit together

A FIRM HAND
Wherever possible, modern conservation is durable but also reversible. The synthetic adhesive used on this jar, was selected with these considerations in mind. A very thin layer of adhesive is applied so as not to distort the re-assembled pot.

Sand allows joined sherds to be supported at the necessary angle

STICKING TOGETHER
The adhesives used in conservation are often quite slow drying so that the conservator has plenty of time to get the join accurate. Pieces of masking tape are taped over at right angles to the join, front and back, to support it while the glue is drying. Masking tape is used because its stretchiness keeps the join under tension.

STANDING IN THE SAND
The joined pieces are put to dry in a tray filled with sand. The gradual reassembly of a pot starts with the rim or the base, whichever is more complete. More masking tape supports the glued joins. Once the glue is completely dry the masking tape can be removed.

As the vessel takes shape, the pieces begin to support each other

A CIRCLE OF SHERDS
Although most pottery from excavations is broken and incomplete, sometimes enough pieces survive from one vessel to make a complete reconstruction. First the sherds are cleaned by gentle washing in water. If they have absorbed salts from the surrounding soil, they are soaked in tapwater which is changed regularly, until all the salts have dissolved out. The sherds are now laid out in order – like a jigsaw puzzle.

Base is often the most resilient part of a pot and so survives well

GETTING PLASTERED

Modern repair and restoration must be unobtrusive, but obvious on close examination. Missing bits in pottery are filled in with plaster of Paris. First a sheet of heated wax is moulded against a part of the inside of the pot – its shape should match that of the missing piece. When the wax cools and hardens it is moved round and fastened with masking tape behind the hole to support the plaster. As soon as the plaster sets the conservator smooths it with a fine scalpel.

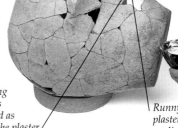

Broken features, such as decorations, spouts, handles, and lugs, are clues to matching up adjacent sherds

Wax backing acts both as support and as mould for the plaster

Runny plaster is gradually applied into the hole

Rimsherds are like the edge pieces of a jigsaw – a good place to start assembling the puzzle

Sherds of a pottery jar from an olive oil factory found at the Jordanian site of Tell es-Sa'idiyeh, c. 2600 B.C., where oil was stored or exported

Spout of vessel

Ring supports jar at any angle during restoration

SPOT THE DIFFERENCE

When the plaster is quite dry its surface is rubbed down with fine abrasive papers, taking care not to scratch the original pot. It is now ready to be painted, using a colour which blends in with, but does not exactly match, the colour of the pot itself. The colour match should look the same at a distance, but close to it should be distinguishable from the pot.

TOGETHER WE STAND

This now complete "hole-mouth" jar was used in making olive oil. Olives, soaked in hot water and crushed, were placed in this jar to settle. The pulp and water would sink to the bottom and the pure olive oil would float to the top, to be poured off through the spout.

Continued on next page

Painstaking processes

Conservation begins with stabilization to minimize further deterioration. The necessary conditions must be provided to ensure the continued well-being of objects. This may involve controlling temperature, humidity, and lighting, and taking precautions against air pollution, mould, and pests. Objects may need to be investigated and cleaned. Some may need to be repaired and restored. The golden rule of modern conservators is that all treatments should be reversible if required – glues must be soluble, mends or patches must be easy to distinguish from the original object and easy to remove, treatments must not chemically alter the object. Modern scientific advances have greatly aided conservators, providing a range of useful synthetic materials, like adhesives, sophisticated tools and techniques for cleaning and consolidating, and a battery of instruments to examine objects. But it is still a slow and painstaking job, as each object has to be treated individually.

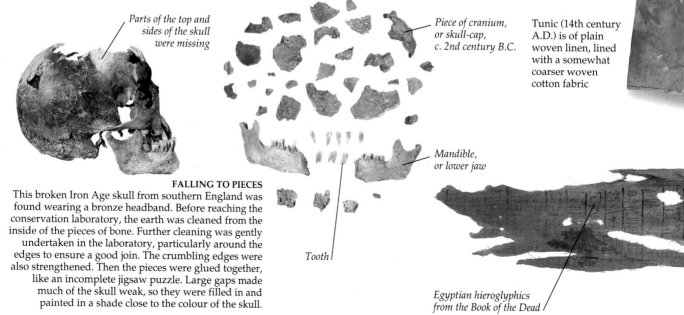

Conserved half of bowl, 1st century A.D.

Unconserved half of copper alloy bowl from the United Arab Emirates

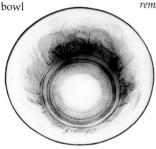

X-ray of corroded bowl

Inside of bowl with most of the surface corrosion removed

A LOOK INSIDE
Machines which can "look into" objects are invaluable to the conservator. X-rays are particularly useful, allowing the conservator to assess the condition and nature of an object. This may be important in determining the treatment it receives, such as the pewter flagon from the *Mary Rose* (pp. 34–35).

COMPLICATED CONSERVATION
X-rays revealed an elaborate and decorative frieze beneath the corroded exterior of this bowl. The decorated surface was revealed by removing the corrosion, fragment by fragment, with a scalpel under a microscope. The contrast with the bowl's half-cleaned exterior is startling. Chemicals are sometimes used to remove corrosion in order to reveal the original surface of metal objects. They were not used on this bowl because they might have damaged the decorated surface.

Parts of the top and sides of the skull were missing

Piece of cranium, or skull-cap, c. 2nd century B.C.

Tunic (14th century A.D.) is of plain woven linen, lined with a somewhat coarser woven cotton fabric

Mandible, or lower jaw

FALLING TO PIECES
This broken Iron Age skull from southern England was found wearing a bronze headband. Before reaching the conservation laboratory, the earth was cleaned from the inside of the pieces of bone. Further cleaning was gently undertaken in the laboratory, particularly around the edges to ensure a good join. The crumbling edges were also strengthened. Then the pieces were glued together, like an incomplete jigsaw puzzle. Large gaps made much of the skull weak, so they were filled in and painted in a shade close to the colour of the skull.

Tooth

Egyptian hieroglyphics from the Book of the Dead

A dark blue striped silk fabric edged the neckline

After turning right way out, the backing was adjusted so that its weave ran parallel to that of the tunic

Curved suture needle makes the task of stitching on a flat surface easier

FRAGILE TEXTILE

This damaged and very brittle linen tunic came to the conservation laboratory inside out. Its fragility meant that it had first to be mounted on a supportive backing made of new cotton cloth, dyed to a colour close to that of the tunic. The backing was sewn to the tunic, with extra stitching around the worst holes, and the tunic was carefully turned right side out. The temporary stitching was removed and the damaged areas repaired with almost invisible stitches using matching silk thread.

BOOK OF THE DEAD

Before conservation, this piece of shroud was a crumpled mass. Water vapour was used to relax the linen, gently separating the fragments. Then the shroud was opened out carefully. The text enabled the pieces to be related correctly, then mounted on to paper.

Heron

Linen shroud
(c. 1450 B.C.)
after conservation

Human remains

THE REMAINS OF HUMAN BODIES give direct evidence of our past. Bones give some information, soft tissue more, and scientific aids, such as CAT scans and microchemical analysis, reveal amazing details. We can find out what people ate, the work they did, how long they lived, and what illnesses they suffered. Inherited physical differences in bone structure are one of several clues to relationships between individuals. Ancient DNA yields important data on human evolution. Even footprints give clues, showing Lucy and her relatives (pp. 6–7) walked upright.

Skin moulded over replica of Ice Man's skull

Pegs mark key points on the skull where thickness of soft tissues is known

Nose cartilege has been added – its shape depends partly on the skull's shape

IN THE FLESH
Soft tissue, preserved in such individuals as the Ice Man who died in the Alps more than 4,000 years ago, is very informative. Stomach contents show what the person's last meal contained. Hair styles and body decoration can survive, as can parasites and traces of viruses. Whole bodies reveal far more about ancient diseases than we can tell just from bones.

GET STUFFED
Ancient Egyptians mummified (artificially preserved) their important dead. The corpse's internal organs were removed and the remaining body preserved by packing crystals of natron (a kind of soda) around it. The body was stuffed with leaves or sawdust to restore the natural contours of the body. Finally, the mummified body was carefully bandaged in linen.

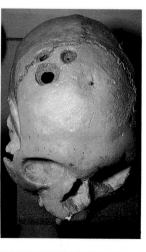

A DRASTIC CURE!
The bizarre practice of trepanning (cutting a disc of bone from a living person's skull), was perhaps used to treat headaches or relieve pressure on brain tumours – many patients survived! Other skeletons show deliberate mutilation to fit society's idea of beauty, such as binding a baby's head to change its shape. Skeletons may also reveal accidental injury or abnormal wear on bones caused by occupational hazards.

FACE TO FACE
We are able to reconstruct what people of the past looked like by using clues from bone structure and our knowledge of anatomy. Another interesting example is the reconstruction of the skull from a richly furnished tomb at Vergina in Greece. Comparison of the reconstructed head with literary sources and portraits identified him as Philip of Macedon, Alexander the Great's father.

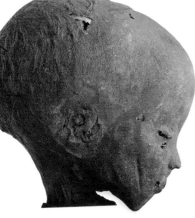

Hair was well preserved by cold, arid econditions

This head is from one of the Arica mummies – mummification was the result of an earthquake

Tooth eruption data for aging show this child was about two years old

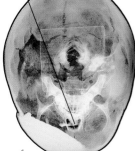

X-ray of Peruvian child's skull

PERUVIAN PEOPLE

A study of skeletons buried at Arica in Peru, c. 5800–2000 B.C., shows it was rare for individuals to live past 50 years old. On average women died before men. Many women had deformed ankle joints, interpreted as showing they had worked in a crouched position. Such work-related stress on a skeleton can often be detected. Archers from the *Mary Rose* (pp. 32–35), for example, showed spinal trauma and thickened forearms.

THE INSIDE STORY

Human teeth emerge and ends of bones fuse at known ages in childhood, so "aging" children's remains is possible. Adults are harder to age, but wear on teeth and structural changes in their skeletons can give some clues. Now new scientific analyses may give a better indication of age.

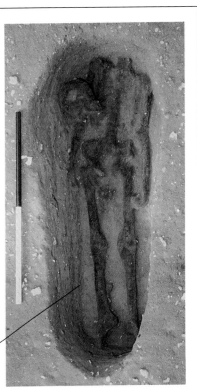

Stain of bones in the sand body fluoresces under ultraviolet light and can be photographed to reveal the skeleton

A GHOST IN THE SAND

It is an amazing fact of modern science that we can study bodies which have disappeared. At Sutton Hoo (pp. 26–27), acid sandy soil has completely destroyed the remains of buried Anglo Saxons – but has left a tell-tale stain in the soil. Some biochemical elements, such as amino acids, survive decay. Even in sand bodies, these can be detected in the soil, revealing the individual's sex and blood group.

Eye colour must be guessed

AN EYE TO THE FUTURE

The Ice Man was accidentally preserved where he died, but most human remains come from burials. Neanderthal skeletons with carefully placed offerings were the first deliberate burials. Neanderthals also cared for their disabled – an individual from Shanidar in Iraq was too cripppled to fend for himself, but survived to old age. Some cultures cremate the dead – surprisingly even cremated remains are very informative. Others expose their dead. Evidence of this in Neolithic Britain comes from the necropolis at Hambledon Hill, where many incomplete skeletons were found, including the lower part of a body, gnawed by dogs.

Skin condition and colour of hair must be guessed, as the skull gives no clues to what these looked like

Food and environment

WHAT DID PEOPLE IN THE PAST EAT? How did they get their food? Obviously, we will never know all the answers to these questions, because most food is eaten and many food remains perish. But archaeologists find clues in their knowledge of what foods were available at the time, which tools might have been used to prepare them, and how modern groups find food. Plant foods do not usually survive, while bones do – this gives us an unbalanced picture of past diet. Although our evidence is incomplete, we can begin to see how people found ways to increase their food supply, using tools and controlling plants and animals. But people are still animals, subject to the laws of nature. Remembering this helps us to understand how our ancestors got their food.

Three fish hooks from Ancient Egypt

SKEWERED SKULL
For most of human existence, people have lived by hunting and gathering wild foods. Plants must have played a major role in the diet of people living in most tropical and temperate areas. Only in harsh arctic environments would meat have constituted the main source of food. But since plant remains do not preserve well, most archaeological evidence is of hunting – like this skull (right).

GETTING HOOKED
Evidence of past diet from food remains can be added to by interpreting the uses of certain artefacts. Further clues come from how worn they were or from residues (such as "silica gloss" on tools used for harvesting plants). These hooks show that fishing occurred, but the harpoons could have been used to hunt a variety of creatures.

Harpoon was fastened to wooden shaft

OLD FISH BONES
Generally fish bones are small and fragile so they, like plant remains, are often under-represented among archaeological finds. Identifying fish bones tells us what species were being eaten and some provide evidence of the time of year when they were caught. Deep-sea species indicate that people had developed boats for offshore navigation.

Central prong was attached to a rope

Three Egyptian harpoons – fish and hippopotami were hunted with such weapons

Fish bones from site in Jordan

Hook formed by mammoth's tail held spear before it was thrown

Tusk

A USEFUL SPEAR-THROWER
Unlike most other animals, people can extend their natural capabilities by devising and using tools. This beautiful carving of a mammoth (c. 12,000 B.C.), made from a reindeer antler, is also part of a useful tool.

ABORIGINAL HUNTER
An Australian Aboriginal is shown using a spear-thrower. By extending the length of his arm, the hunter's spear-thrower allows the spear to be propelled with greater force over a longer distance. By observing such artefacts in use, archaeologists have been able to identify and interpret artefacts from the past, such as the Palaeolithic spear-thrower (far left).

Carts, sleds, or ploughs could carry loads or people and be pulled by bullocks, horses, llamas, even dogs

MORE THAN JUST MEAT

Animals provided more than just meat. Hides were made into leather, and wool or hair into textiles. Cows, ewes, goats, and even horses gave milk for drinking and to make cheese, butter, and yoghurt. The proportions of male and female, and young and old animals on archaeological sites indicate the purposes for which they were kept.

Bos primigenius
Burwell Fen

3

Neolithic axe killed this aurochs about 4,000 years ago

Eye socket

MOUNDS OF MOLLUSCS

Shell middens are mounds of discarded mollusc shells, but include other food remains. Although the amounts of shells were large, the food value was small. One red deer gives more calories than 50,000 oysters! Molluscs were a useful standby for lean periods in seasonally varied diets.

SHEPHERDING

In many parts of the world, the last 10,000 years have seen a shift from hunting animals to herding them. Domestication and the spread of farming communities took many animals far from their original homes – Indian jungle fowl to Europe, for example, and Western Asiatic goats to India.

Soay sheep is a primitive breed – its wool, shed naturally in early summer, was plucked, not sheared

Skull of an aurochs (*Bos primigenius*), ancestor of our domestic cattle

Butchery mark

BUTCHERED BONES

Excavated bones may be fragmentary, but the species of animal they came from can often be identified. Details of shape and development may allow the age and sex of the animals to be determined, resulting in a picture of the way they were managed – for meat, milk, wool, traction, or transport. These animal bones from Jordan show butchery marks where foot bones were cut off leg bones.

Continued on next page

Carbonized wheat, barley, fig seeds, and grape pips

Environmental findings

Local weather and environment have always played an important part in conditions of life. Archaeologists are interested in reconstructing the climate, vegetation, and other environmental aspects of the past – their studies range from personal hygiene to global climatic change. Some aspects of climate and environment have left marks on the landscape such as great valleys carved by glaciers, or ancient beaches left high and dry by changes in sea level. Others can be reconstructed using micro-organisms from sediments deep in the sea. Soils reflect the conditions in which they were formed, and many small creatures live only in restricted environments. Combined with evidence from plant remains, these sources allow vegetation, rainfall, temperature, soils, human influences, and other aspects of environments (both local and global) to be reconstructed.

GROW MORE FOOD
Human population has grown through the ages because we have found ways to control and increase our food supply, including agriculture. Grains, husks, and other bits of plant, such as the remains, above, from a site in Jordan, show that many early farmers grew cereals – wheat, barley, maize, millet, or rice. Probably root crops were equally important in many areas, but they leave no archaeological traces.

TOO TEMPTING
Other plant foods were important to early farmers. Central America lacked animals that were suitable for domestication, so beans were a vital source of protein. Initially farmers used local plants, but gradually cultivated plants were introduced from other areas. Often agriculture became increasingly intensive, productivity rising along with the amount of work involved. Population growth may have encouraged this. Greater food supplies also supported trade and industry.

Pomegranates were popular in ancient Egypt

This species of land snail lived on chalky downland

CRAWLING WITH INFORMATION
Microscopic animals from water-logged deposits at York in northern England show aspects of personal hygiene and daily life. One Roman sewer contained flies from toilets, as well as the type of beetle that lived in stored grain, showing that the sewer had drained a granary. Waste from tanning leather was found in York's Viking settlement, including dung beetles (above). In cesspits (pp. 6–7) were parasite eggs showing that worms had infested people's intestines.

FUSSY SNAILS
Past vegetation, soils, and climate can be reconstructed from various plant and animal remains. Land snails prefer very specific habitats, so they are excellent indicators of local environment. Changes through time are reflected by changes in the snail population. Beetles, insects, and tiny mammals also give a picture of conditions on land, while aquatic diatoms (single-celled algae) reflect conditions in lakes and pools.

Pairs of crossed rods and a rail supported a series of planks

THE HAND OF MAN

Ancient charcoal shows hunter-gatherers used fire to make forest clearings, attracting animals to hunt, and encouraging edible plants to grow. Pollen shows changes in vegetation when agriculture was introduced to an area, with trees giving way to cultivated plants and their weeds. The Sweet Track in the Somerset Levels of south-western England was built from trackways of hurdles woven from hazel rods about 5,000 years ago. This shows that hazel was being coppiced (cut right down to encourage growth). Woodland management was well developed by these farmers. The Sweet Track also yielded beetles, indicating that when it was built the winters were colder and the summers hotter than nowadays.

UNSAVOURY INTEREST

Human coprolites (preserved faeces) show what people ate. Dissected examples contain bits of plant and bone, and eggs of infesting parasites. Animal coprolites give similar information about their diet, which may also give an insight into local vegetation.

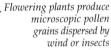

Dog coprolites – some are found in water-logged cesspits, others in dry areas

LOST OPPORTUNITIES

Many areas were once inhabited but are no longer. Sometimes the change is due to human activity – over-exploitation, deforestation, or salination caused by irrigation. Elsewhere there may be natural causes as when rivers changed course and farmers followed them. Rock paintings in the Sahara show domestic cattle that required a much moister habitat. Environmental evidence shows this region once supported woodland, grassland, and lakes, but dried up from 6000 B.C. onwards.

Flowering plants produce microscopic pollen grains dispersed by wind or insects

Pollen grains of a pine tree

Pollen grains of plantain (a type of weed)

MICROSCOPIC BEAUTY

Pollen grains give clues for environmental and climatic reconstruction at all levels. In domestic situations, pollen relates to plant foods being eaten at that time. Pollen from soil samples reflects local ecology, while pollen samples from lakes or bogs give a picture of vegetation over a wider region. Changes through time in trees and plants can indicate shifts in vegetation because of human activities or climatic change. Widely fluctuating global climate in the last two and half million years has been reconstructed from deep-sea deposits and long pollen records, and their results broadly agree.

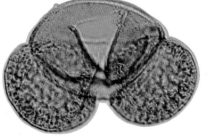

Investigating daily life

ARCHAEOLOGY PLAYS A MAJOR ROLE in understanding the past. What do artefacts such as these finds from Roman Britain tell us? Some information is straightforward. Analyses of artefacts tell much about ancient technology. Often what the artefacts were used for can be determined by microscopic investigations revealing food residues or patterns of wear. Certain objects discovered together or in a particular context can also help in understanding their use. Archaeologists wish to find out about other aspects of the past, such as social organization, but evidence for these are harder to interpret.

FASHIONABLE FOOTWEAR
Fashion has always influenced the clothes people wear, but rarely are archaeologists able to recover ancient clothing. They have to be content with artistic representations, and small surviving fittings such as belt or shoe buckles, or the jewellery used to fasten cloaks or tunics.

Leather clothing preserved in a water-logged site

Roman-style sandal cut from a single piece of leather

These 1st-2nd century A.D. manacles show that slave trading continued under Roman rule

ON A PLATE
The Romans used metal as well as pottery for tableware, such as this plate. People ate with fingers, the point of a knife, or a spoon (such as this 1st-2nd century A.D. pewter example) – forks were a much later invention. Food remains add to the knowledge of Roman eating habits which we have from such literary sources as the famous cookery book by Apicius. Oyster shells are a very common find from Roman Britain.

Oysters were a cheap food in England up to the 1800s when they were destroyed by disease

ENSLAVED
Roman literary sources mention Britain as an important source of slaves, even before the conquest in A.D. 43. Finds of iron slave manacles and chains with neck rings vividly confirm the reality of this British export. Not all slaves endured harsh conditions. Many were valued members of the family circle and were eventually freed or bought their freedom with their savings.

The value of typology

Typological classification is important in archaeologists' work. Taking a group of pots, an archaeologist asks, "How can I divide these up to find out more about them and the society they belonged to?" Differences in pots' clays, shapes, decoration, and manufacturing techniques, can be examined. Style changes are useful for dating, types from different places indicate trade, and variations in quality can show social status.

Clay used to manufacture mortaria had pieces of grit added to produce the desired rough surface

MIXING IT
A *mortarium* (or mixing bowl) was a common feature of the Romano-British kitchen. Its gritty surface was useful for grinding ingredients into powder. Its large size could hold a considerable quantity of ingredients for mixing together and its pouring lip helped in removing the completed mixture – sausages, perhaps.

TOP QUALITY
Technically perfect, samian was Roman Britain's top luxury tableware. Manufactured mainly in Gaul (France), samian was made in elaborate moulds. Often the maker's name was stamped on the base. A very clear picture of the organization both of the industrial production of samian and the wide distribution network is formed by studying the accumulated evidence of these names.

Name of maker (Igocatus) is stamped on the base of this samian bowl found in London, England

*Amphorae were stacked
horizontally in transit –
when in use they
were propped
against a wall*

POTS OF STORAGE
Some pottery travelled
around the ancient world
as disposable or re-useable
containers, similar to our glass
or plastic bottles. They provide
evidence for those commodities
they were designed to carry.
Amphorae (tall tapering pottery
jars) were used in the Roman
world to transport not only dry
goods, but also wine, olive oil,
and garum – a sauce made from
fermented fish frequently used
to season cooking.

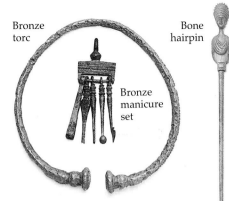

Bronze
torc

Bronze
manicure
set

Bone
hairpin

CHANGING FASHIONS
Long bone hairpins were used in elaborate
Roman hairstyles of the 1st century A.D.
(above). Later, shorter pins showed
hairstyles had become simpler. A bronze
manicure set was worn on a Roman lady's
belt – the quality and decoration show it
was a prized personal ornament.

A ROMAN KITCHEN
This Roman kitchen was reconstructed using both historical
and archaeological evidence. Many
humbler wares, such as a *mortarium*,
coarse vessels and amphorae, glass
storage jars, and some kitchen
utensils, were frequent finds on
Roman settlement sites. Bones and
plant residues from excavations
combined with documentary and
pictorial evidence give us a good
picture of what Romans ate.

COOKING POT
Most Roman pottery was mass produced
and often travelled considerable distances
from manufacturer to user. Many different
types of coarse cooking pots were used,
mainly locally made. This greyware
was made in southeast England and
used in Roman London.

*Carrot-shaped
amphora stored
dry foods – an
analysis of
residues from
one amphora
showed traces
of wheat flour*

*Pot would
have been set in
embers to cook food*

*Nene Valley "hunt
cups" were often
decorated with
hunting scenes*

*Tapering form of the
amphora makes it easy
to lift and balance on
the shoulder, but
handles were weak*

*Nene Valley
potteries first
began to supply
the demands of
the locally-based
military, shortly
after the conquest
of Britain in A.D. 43*

NENE VALLEY WARE
England's Nene Valley, with good
clays, plenty of timber, and a well-
developed road and water transport
network, became one of the main pottery
manufacturing areas in Roman Britain.
One of the main products of these potteries
was Nene Valley ware, a fine tableware
decorated with semi-liquid clay applied like
cake icing – a cheaper alternative to samian.

Clues to trade and industry

SCIENCE PROVIDES MANY TOOLS for understanding how trade and industry were carried out in the past. For example, chemical and physical analyses of metal spears can show us which ores they were made from, where these ores came from, and their makers' skills and technological knowledge. Even the source of the stone used to make a prehistoric axe, or the clay to make a Roman pot, can be identified by scientific analysis. Matching artefacts to their source in this way is a complex process, but it is a rewarding one, for it tells archaeologists much about how societies traded with each other to obtain the raw materials they needed or the luxuries they wanted. The pattern of these trade links also provides information about how the societies involved related to each other, and how they were organized.

Mace wrapped around nutmeg

Nutmeg

ALONG THE SPICE ROUTE
Nowadays food can be preserved for long periods by freezing. Other methods, such as salting or drying, were necessary until recently so food was often uninteresting or unpalatable. Spices could disguise such tastes and so were highly prized. Since many were acquired from distant lands, they were expensive and often traded for gold.

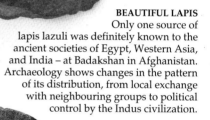

BEAUTIFUL LAPIS
Only one source of lapis lazuli was definitely known to the ancient societies of Egypt, Western Asia, and India – at Badakshan in Afghanistan. Archaeology shows changes in the pattern of its distribution, from local exchange with neighbouring groups to political control by the Indus civilization.

Simple, one-piece mould for making early cast objects

Simple flat axe

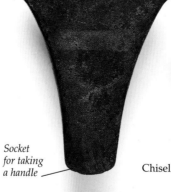

Socket for taking a handle

Chisel

Tiny blade of obsidian (natural volcanic glass)

Flint tools (centre, right)

FITTING THE MOULD
Copper was first used as an attractive "stone" with the unusual property of changing shape when hammered. People then began to heat and smelt copper and to alloy it with other minerals, such as arsenic, antimony, tin, and lead, to improve aspects of its performance. Early objects in copper or bronze often imitated the shape of familiar stone objects. Bronze tools and weapons eventually largely superceded stone ones, but they were initially more important as status symbols.

GRIMES GRAVES
Flint mining and stone quarrying began early in the Neolithic period as demand grew for axes to clear forests for agriculture. Often small-scale, there were also some much larger examples, such as Grimes Graves mines in eastern England.

NATURAL GLASS
Obsidian was prized by past societies in Western Asia, Europe, and Central America. Using scientific analysis to match obsidian artefacts with restricted sources of the glass shows how it was traded among prehistoric groups.

A wooden or clay stopper prevented air getting in to spoil the contents inside the amphora

Large handle for lifting heavy amphora

THE SILK ROUTE
The Chinese controlled the lively trade route to the west through the inhospitable Central Asian desert. Indian Buddhism spread along this route to China. These far-flung trade and cultural relations come together in this painting – a 9th-century A.D. Chinese silk scroll showing a Buddhist figure holding a glass vessel of Persian origin.

Painting was found by Sir Aurel Stein at Tun-huang in China

Sassanian glass bowl (c. 500 A.D.)

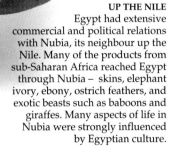

Pottery vessel, a typical Nubian type exported to Egypt, 16th-century B.C.

ANOTHER AMPHORA
Surviving wrecks of Roman ships carrying amphorae give a good picture of the way in which trade was conducted in Roman times. Amphorae often bore the name of their manufacturer. Often other stamps indicated their contents which can sometimes be verified today by chemical analysis of the food residues inside the containers.

UP THE NILE
Egypt had extensive commercial and political relations with Nubia, its neighbour up the Nile. Many of the products from sub-Saharan Africa reached Egypt through Nubia – skins, elephant ivory, ebony, ostrich feathers, and exotic beasts such as baboons and giraffes. Many aspects of life in Nubia were strongly influenced by Egyptian culture.

EGYPTIAN TRADE
Wall paintings, texts, and archaeological finds show how extensive Egypt's trade relations were. Here 15th-century B.C. envoys from Syria bring goods to Egypt. Objects came from as far away as Minoan Crete – cedarwood for ship building was a major import from Lebanon. Punt, a mysterious land on the Red Sea, supplied incense. Turquoise and copper were mined in the Sinai Desert.

Buildings of the past

MANY BUILDINGS OF THE PAST have disappeared, but others still stand thousands of years later. Many factors govern survival – the building material used (perishable wood or durable stone), the structure's function (permanent religious buildings or overnight shelters), and subsequent activities in the area (undisturbed desert tombs or houses in an ever changing city). Various factors also determine whether we can trace past structures. Postholes show the foundations of timber buildings, but those built directly on the ground are gone forever unless the position of finds inside and out reveals where they once stood. Objects are recovered in excavations, but structures are destroyed – postholes dug out or walls removed to expose the layers underneath. All structural information must be recorded carefully in notes, plans, photographs, and sections, since these records are all that will remain.

ANCIENT PEOPLE AT HOME
Our early ancestors' structures are rarely preserved, so the chances of finding them are tiny. The discovery, at Terra Amata in France, of a hut 300,000 years old was incredible luck. Stake holes show it was built of brushwood, with stones around the outside and stouter posts holding up the roof. The hut collapsed after it was abandoned, but was rebuilt when people returned in the spring.

Victorian building, partially demolished

A PEEPHOLE INTO THE PAST
Successful towns are occupied for centuries, each generation building over the remains of the previous ones. Their early stages are hard to investigate because the modern town gets in the way. When structures are demolished for redevelopment, archaeologists can examine small pieces of the town underneath, from which they construct a patchwork picture of the past. This model shows one such excavated "peephole" into old London.

Deposits that have accumulated since medieval times

Fence enclosing building site in 1881–1882 when this area in London's Gracechurch Street was cleared to build Leadenhall Market

Walls of medieval Leadenhall – in medieval times, London was a major industrial centre and international port

Remains of Roman basilica, incorporated into medieval Leadenhall

ETERNAL DEATH
Houses may last a lifetime, but monumental tombs are for eternity. These Egyptian pyramids at Giza, built to house dead pharaohs through a perpetual afterlife, have endured nearly 5,000 years. They are a monument now to their labourers who dragged and levered the massive blocks into place.

PEOPLE UNDERFOOT
Buildings when excavated often seem constructed of plain brick or bare stone. But originally they were not so stark. Many houses had painted plaster walls, such as those that survive in Roman Pompeii, along with exquisite floor mosaics, here showing actors preparing for a play.

FULLY FURNISHED
Skara Brae on Orkney, Scotland gives a rare glimpse inside a Neolithic furnished house, c. 3000 B.C. Timber was scarce on the island, so Skara Brae's builders constructed all the normal furnishings in stone. A freak sandstorm engulfed the settlement, preserving the houses undisturbed, complete with stone shelves, beds, hearths, and even water tanks for keeping shellfish fresh.

COMPUTER WIZARDRY
The remains of Cluny, the great 11th-century French abbey, were meticulously excavated between 1928 and 1950. In 1990–1991 engineering students working at IBM successfully reconstructed Cluny with a computer, using the excavation records and special software designed for architects. Computer-generated imagery can accurately recreate vanished buildings, but only if the data is sufficient. Evidence for prehistoric structures is often limited to ground plans, but computers can test different reconstructions – an alternative to actually building them (pp. 58–59)!

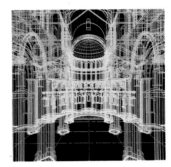

Reconstructing Cluny by computer beginning (above) and end (top)

Public buildings, such as this Roman basilica, are often created in enduring materials, such as brick or stone, which survive better than flimsy domestic architecture

Roman arch

Ground surface in 1881–1882

Dating the past

ARCHAEOLOGICAL SITES AND OBJECTS are mainly dated by combining stratigraphy (giving a sequence) and typology (identifying artefacts typical of different periods in the sequence). Except in areas with historical records, archaeologists had only this elastic relative chronology until 1949, when the invention of radiocarbon dating made it possible to date organic remains and thence the deposits they came from. Many more scientific dating techniques have since appeared. Most are radiometric, based on the rate of decay of particular radioactive isotopes. Material is dated by measuring how much of its original radioactive content has decayed since the radiometric "clock" was reset to zero. Dating our early ancestors, like *Homo habilis*, well beyond radiocarbon's range, combines several techniques such as K/Ar, fission track dating, reversals in the Earth's magnetic polarity, and biostratigraphy.

Tree rings grow annually – in sensitive trees like oak, rings vary in thickness from year to year, depending on growing conditions

TREE RING DATING
Fluctuations in the level of C-14 in the atmosphere cause radiocarbon dates, particularly before 1000 B.C., to work out more recent than they really should be. Dendrochronology (tree-ring dating) has helped solve this problem. Using many trees, scientists have built up tree-ring sequences going back beyond 7500 B.C. By comparing radiocarbon dates on wood with its true age known from dendrochronology, scientists have produced a chart converting radiocarbon dates to actual calendar dates.

A REVOLUTION!
Radiocarbon (C-14) is a radioactive isotope that forms a tiny fraction of the carbon in the atmosphere. When living things die, this radiocarbon decays at a known rate. By measuring how much radiocarbon remains in organic material, such as bone, shell, wood, and other plant material, scientists can calculate how long ago death occurred.

Benzene from the conversion process is dated by liquid scintillation counting

SCINTILLATING
To radiocarbon date a bone, a sample is crushed and added to acid to extract the protein (above). This is chemically cleaned and converted to benzene for liquid scintillation counting. The amount of carbon present when the creature died is measured, using the stable isotopes C-12 and C-13. This allows calculation of the amount of C-14 originally present which is compared with the amount still remaining. The proportion which has decayed allows a date to be worked out. An alternative method of measuring uses an acceleration mass spectrometer (AMS). This measures directly the amounts of the different carbon isotopes present, in small samples of material, and can date back to 100,000 B.C.

Material being converted to benzene for dating was once living tissue

Section of a vacuum line – used to convert samples to benzene

HOW OLD IS EARLY MAN?

The remains of man's early ancestors lie far beyond the date range of radiocarbon. Radiometric methods such as potassium-argon dating (K/Ar) and fission-track dating, which date igneous rocks, provide an indirect date for archaeological material in the layers between the rocks. Biostratigraphy is more direct – dated forms in the evolution of such animals as pigs indicate the approximate age of associated archaeological material.

Skull of our early ancestor, *Homo habilis*

ELECTRONS ON THE MOVE

Tiny quantities of radioactive matter occur in the clay used for making pottery. Radioactive decay causes electrons in the pottery structure to be dislodged. These are caught in the crystal lattice of the pot's fabric, where they remain until heated above 500°C (932°F). This took place when the pot was fired, "resetting" the radiometric "clock" to zero. Measuring the extent to which the process of electron displacement has reoccurred allows the date of the pot's firing to be calculated.

Photomultiplier tube

The decorative figures on this terracotta were made using a genuine Zapotec mould, but the figure looked wrong and attracted suspicion of forgery

SEEING THE LIGHT

A small sample is drilled from pottery to be dated by thermoluminescence (TL). This is crushed and sieved to extract quartz crystals, which are placed on a heater plate (above) and put into a photomultiplier machine. When the electrons pop back into place, light is given off. The amount of light is proportional to the age of the pottery and to the amount of radioactive material present.

Drill hole in terracotta statue from which a tiny sample has been taken for TL dating

IS IT ORIGINAL?

Pottery is the most common material found in archaeological sites of the last 10,000 years. So thermoluminescence (TL), the recently developed technique for dating pottery, is a godsend for archaeologists and is invaluable for detecting forgeries (pp. 56–57). For example, the abundance of Zapotec terracottas has aroused suspicion. Using TL to date when these figures were made has revealed that many known examples, including this seated god, are recent fakes.

1981-4-16-1

Fakes and forgeries

THE PURPOSE OF FAKING (fraudulently modifying) and forgery (making falsely) is to deceive. Usually this is done for money: making imitations of valuable, but scarce, antiquities and selling them as genuine. Forged documents, from medieval monastic charters to wills and passports, are used to support claims to land, property, identity, or power. Sometimes eccentric individuals make forgeries for the satisfaction of fooling the experts. Some forgeries are crude copies, while others are sophisticated replicas using ancient technology. The skills developed for conservation can be fraudulently misused to restore damaged objects or put together unrelated broken objects (pastiche), to sell as genuine undamaged antiquities.

IN THE UNDERWORLD
Small shabti figures were placed in Egyptian tombs as substitutes for the deceased in the Underworld. Now many forgeries cast in moulds have supplemented genuine ones and are easily detected by stylistic inaccuracies and nonsensical inscriptions.

COPY CAT!
Differences between ancient and more recent technology can be used to distinguish forgeries from genuine antiquities. Research into ancient methods has enabled skilled forgers to produce technically convincing objects (far right). These can still be identified as forgeries, however, through using scientific techniques like thermoluminescence (pp. 54–55).

AUTHENTIC OR NOT?
This soapstone figure is said to be from Great Zimbabwe in Africa, where similar but larger soapstone columns are known. It is uncertain whether this figure is genuine; it is suspiciously unworn and has no details of when and where it was found. Such information is vital to show the authenticity of doubtful objects.

Red background produced by firing in air

Genuine Athenian black-figure ware vase, 6th century B.C.

During firing, the air supply was reduced and the vessel turned black. When air was reintroduced, painted areas stayed black and the rest turned red

Modern forgery using same methods of production as similar vase (left)

Brown/black "hare's fur" glaze

Fake teabowl

**MODERN FORGERY
VS. ANCIENT ARTEFACT**
The differences between the colourings and glazes on these two teabowls from China is apparent even to the naked eye. The genuine article (right), in dark brown stoneware, has a much more subtle colouring with delicate "hare's fur" markings on its black glaze. The modern forgery (above) has a shiny glaze with similar but crude markings. The base of the forgery has a well-defined shape, while that of the real artefact is roughly joined to the bowl.

Delicate markings on black glaze

Jian ware teabowl from the Song Dynasty (A.D. 960–1279)

Colour of clay is distinctive on this genuine terracotta

Fake terracotta figure of a woman

Genuine terracotta figure of a woman

Drapery is clumsy imitation of genuine terracotta

SPANISH BULL

Assessing the authenticity of ancient works depends on what society knows and expects at the time of their discovery. Archaeologists in the 1800s viewed Palaeolithic people as uncultured savages, so they were scornful of Marcelino de Sautuola's claim in 1879 to have discovered magnificent Palaeolithic paintings at a cave in Altamira in northeastern Spain. They even suggested that the art was forged with his knowledge. De Sautuola's inspired claim for their antiquity was vindicated only after his death with further discoveries of cave art.

TANAGRAS

Despite extensive 19th-century plundering of ancient tombs, demand for fine pieces of classical sculpture was so great that forgeries abounded. Tanagras (draped female figures from the 3rd to 2nd century B.C.) were particularly popular. Their diversity has made it difficult to assess their authenticity on stylistic grounds, as many fakes were skilfully put together from unrelated ancient fragments and sold as "restorations".

16th-century forgery of a sestertius of Claudius

Contemporary counterfeit sestertius, c. A.D. 50

COUNTERFEIT

Despite severe penalties, counterfeiting of official coinage is widespread. Counterfeiters often faked high value coinage by coating a base-metal core in silver or gold. These ancient fakes are detected by careful analysis of their chemical composition. Generally official coins are die-struck, but forgeries are made using a new die, details differing slightly from the original. An identical copy can be produced by making a mould from a genuine coin in which copies are cast. The resulting detail is less sharp than the original.

Genuine sestertius, c. A.D. 42 , of Claudius, Roman emperor from A.D. 41–54

Experimental archaeology

WHEN ARCHAEOLOGISTS INTERPRET their discoveries, they often are trying to make intelligent guesses from what they already know, from their own experience and imagination. Two helpful ways to test their guesses and discover new possibilities are by experimenting (trying out different possibilities) and by ethnographic analogy (looking at how other cultures do things). These approaches not only show that some interpretations do not work while others do, but they may also pinpoint what archaeologists might usefully look for in the future.

A GLASTONBURY HOUSE
This unfinished roundhouse shows coppiced hazel rods (wattle) woven between uprights set in postholes and then plastered with daub (mud, clay, cow dung, hay, and water). The roof had to be pitched at an angle between 45° and 50° to ensure that rainwater would run off, rather than soak the thatch.

Ash flail for separating grain from husks

Flail used for threshing, but experiments showed some early breeds of wheat were difficult to thresh

Shaft for harnessing horse or ox behind vallus to push it through crop

Box contained wooden spears, which broke the stalks and collected the grain

Vallus (Celtic reaping machine)

Rafters bound to ring tie-beam support thatch

Iron rim applied when red-hot to tighten up the wheel (made of elm, oak, or ash) as iron contracted

TOOLS OF THE TRADE
Actual archaeological evidence of Iron Age farming is limited, although Roman records show that Iron Age Britain was prosperous, exporting grain and hides. Work at the experimental Butser Ancient Farm in England has helped fill some of the gaps in our knowledge, demonstrating the efficiency of Iron Age implements. The ard was shown to be suitable for working not only light soils but, contrary to expectation, heavy clay soils as well.

Beam of ard went between the pair of oxen and was attached to the yoke

Ard, made of ash, was an early type of plough drawn by a pair of oxen

Handle held by ploughman to keep the share correctly angled in the ground

Share for ripping through the ground but not turning it, unlike a true plough

LIFE IN THE ROUND
Much of the work at Butser has focused on reconstructing an Iron Age roundhouse. Archaeologists know it had a ring of postholes surrounded by an outer ring of stakeholes. What structure using this set-up would be stable and durable? How was the roof made? This experimental reconstruction helped answer such questions. This large roundhouse is built of ash and oak uprights, interspersed by hazel wattling, plastered with daub, and roofed with thatch on a framework of radial wooden rafters interwoven with hazel rods, like a spider's web.

ETHNOARCHAEOLOGY

Ethnographic evidence is very valuable because it not only shows archaeologists the many ways different people make artefacts and provide shelter, clothing, and food, but also gives some insight into other aspects of their lives. However, modern ethnography cannot tell us exactly how the past worked – no two cultures are the same and modern cultures are not "living fossils" of our ancestors' way of life. Much can be learned about stone tool technology from Australia's Aboriginals, who use traditional methods on many modern materials.

Cap kept in smoke, but kept out rain, birds, and insects

Old English game fowl were bred from Indian jungle fowl

Lancehead made from beer-bottle glass

Arrowhead made from telegraph insulator

Arrowhead made from coloured glass

Ears of einkorn, one of the earliest wheats cultivated

Grains of einkorn

PRIMITIVE BREEDS

Butser has a range of primitive breeds – cattle, five kinds of sheep, and these Old English game fowl – as similar as possible to ones kept in the Iron Age. Work with these animals highlights aspects of their behaviour which would have affected Iron Age farmers – like the difficulty of confining Soay sheep, given their ability to jump fences. Ploughing experiments using small, strong Dexter cattle show their ability to plough much larger areas in a day than had previously been expected.

CULTIVATING THE PAST

Experimental cultivation of different cereal grains grown in the Iron Age gives interesting information on yields, disease resistance, weed and weather tolerances, and nutritional content. At Butser, important experiments have also been done on grain storage, showing the suitability of underground storage in sealed pits, a common feature of Iron Age sites.

Porch roof thatched with wheat straw

Massive porch based on an excavated plan of an actual Iron Age house

Industrial archaeology

Aᴿᴄʜᴀᴇᴏʟᴏɢʏ ɪs ᴀs ᴍᴜᴄʜ ᴀʙᴏᴜᴛ ᴛᴏᴅᴀʏ – a lost key, a discarded plastic bag – as about the remote past. Over the last 300 years, there have been huge advances in making things – industrial archaeology is the study of that technological heritage. Major industrial advances, like Abraham Darby's innovative use of coke to smelt iron (1709), are well-known. But even the best-known industrial processes have unrecorded details, while much experimental work and many unspectacular industries have fallen into obscurity, from which archaeology can rescue them. Trivial everyday details that fascinate us now were essential knowledge to the artisans of the time.

FLOATING TRANSPORT
Good communications are vital to industry, bringing in raw materials and distributing finished products. Until railways revolutionized land transport in the mid 19th century, water was the only means of carrying low-value, bulky commodities. During the 1700s, canals were built to improve and extend the available water transport network.

GOING LIKE A ROCKET
Modern railways have their origins in wooden, and later iron, rails laid for moving heavy hand- and horse-drawn wagons. By the late 1700s, there was a great need for reliable, all-season transport. Stationary steam engines were becoming an important alternative to water power. Attempts were made to devise a steam-powered moving engine to replace animal traction. In 1802, Richard Trevithick ran the first steam locomotive in the world.

George and Robert Stephensons' 1829 prizewinning *Rocket* locomotive was efficient and reliable, unlike its rivals

PIT WINDING GEAR
There was a great expansion in English coal mining during the 1600s. At later mines, like this one at Ironbridge, winding gear (operated by horse, then steam) brought coal to the surface. Archaeological research has done much to reveal details of the early history of coal mining. Today it is hard to appreciate the dreadful conditions under which many miners worked.

Huge, bottle-shaped kiln provided an updraught to keep temperature inside to 1250°C (2282°F)

CHINA WORKS
From the mid 1700s, several potteries in the Ironbridge Gorge, the centre of the Industrial Revolution in England, began manufacturing imitations of expensive Chinese porcelain using china clay imported from the south-west. Archaeological work in this area has documented the changing fortunes of the different potteries, providing much information on less prestigious local ceramics and the domestic lives of potters and other residents there.

THE IRON BRIDGE
The River Severn provided transport for industries developing on both sides of the Ironbridge Gorge, but it impeded local movement. The problem of bridging it was solved by building in iron. The world's first iron bridge, opened in 1781, was a splendid advertisement for the strength and versatility of cast iron, and an instant tourist sight. It made industry, especially iron-working, attractive to the layman and exciting to the entrepreneur.

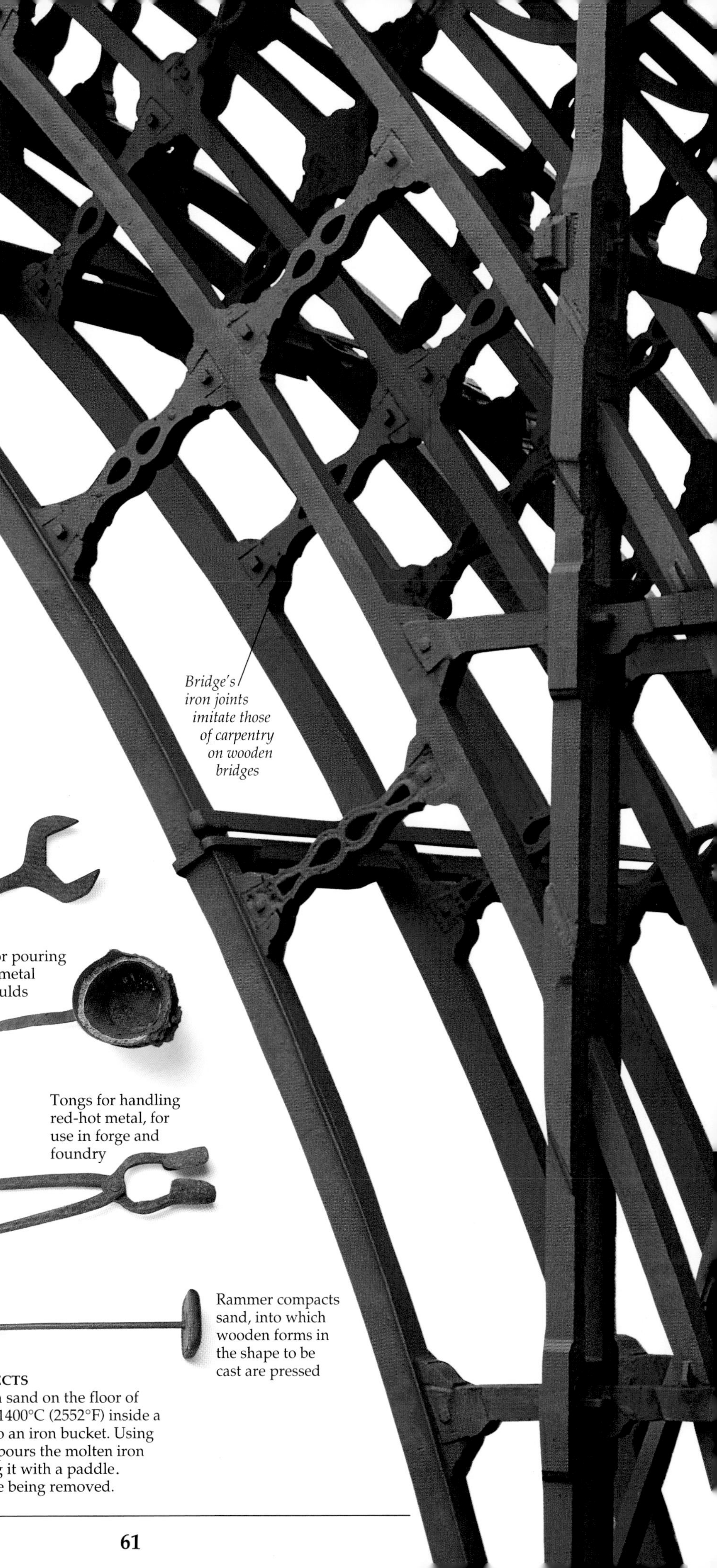

Pouring molten iron into sand mould

Padded gloves for protection

WHAT A BLAST!
Blast furnaces like Bedlam at Ironbridge produced "pigs" of cast iron, for casting or for working into wrought iron. The only remaining British producer of wrought iron is Ironbridge's Blists Hill. It operates as a living museum demonstrating many industrial, commercial, and domestic activities of the last century.

Bridge's iron joints imitate those of carpentry on wooden bridges

Small ladle

Hot cutter for cutting hot iron in the forge

Spanner, or wrench

Ladle for pouring molten metal into moulds

Tongs for handling red-hot metal, for use in forge and foundry

Rammer compacts sand, into which wooden forms in the shape to be cast are pressed

Spike for making holes in sand to release air as hot metal is poured into mould

CASTING IRON OBJECTS
Specially shaped moulds are made in sand on the floor of the foundry. Pig iron is heated to about 1400°C (2552°F) inside a small furnace releasing molten iron into an iron bucket. Using a long-handled ladle, the iron-maker pours the molten iron into the waiting moulds, levelling it with a paddle. The castings are left to cool before being removed.

Past into future

WHY INVESTIGATE THE PAST? Everyone is born curious and the past is a natural source of interest and wonder. It is also vitally important. For cultural groups today, their own past reinforces a sense of national identity. At many levels, a knowledge of the past can help us today – for example, archaeological work in such regions as Peru shows how earlier agricultural practices can yield better, more sustainable results than modern ones. But the importance of the past goes beyond this. The past, like the present, is created by individuals who acknowledge links at many levels – not only to their community but to humanity in general. The past belongs to everyone, uniting us in our human ancestry, giving us pride in our achievements as a species, and teaching us universal lessons. It is therefore essential that we ensure the survival of the relics of our past, threatened today as never before.

Vivid colours characterize Palaeolithic paintings at Lascaux's caves in southwestern France – having survived for over 12,000 years, many are now threatened

Elaborate headdress

HEADING FOR TROUBLE
Who owns the past – individual groups or everyone? In such areas as North America and Australia, the physical and cultural remains of native peoples' direct ancestors were plundered in earlier days. Often such cultural material has a living place in native traditions and, quite rightly, much has been returned to their descendants. The question becomes more controversial as we go further back in time or deal with areas whose past involves many cultural groups. The issue is a sensitive one and arouses strong feelings.

Mould growth, caused by visitors' breath upsetting environmental balance, damaged the paintings

Thin section of stone object as seen under a microscope

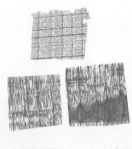

Slide showing anatomy of a beech tree including its tree rings

Bronze head from Benin in West Africa

UNDER THE MICROSCOPE
Science today gives us many ways to investigate the past. Analyzing of stone, pottery, or metal artefacts provides information on how they were made and where their raw materials came from. Scientific dating techniques are vitally important. Science also greatly helps conserve and investigate organic materials, like human remains.

SLIVERS OF INFORMATION
Trees' annual growth rings give a calendar to date past wooden structures precisely. They also yield environmental information, since the width of tree rings relates to annual variations in temperature and soil moisture. Archaeology today investigates every aspect of the past and involves many other fields of study.

Running horse and other Lascaux paintings had to be protected, so caves have been closed to visitors

THE RUNAWAY PAST

Discovering the past may cause its destruction. Although excavation reveals artefacts from the past, it destroys their physical context except on paper where reality is transformed into records (pp. 24–25). Much of the past survived because of unusual conditions which discovery destroys. To prevent the material's decay, its conditions of preservation must be artifically maintained or restored – for example, some of the wood from Somerset Levels has been redeposited in undrained peat in a nature reserve (pp. 46–47).

An exact replica of Lascaux's painted caves, including this horse, has been created for people to visit – a novel solution

ARCHAEOLOGY AND THE PUBLIC

Fieldwalking and rescue excavation have always benefited enormously from the contribution of amateurs. Many archaeological organizations now encourage public participation, especially by schoolchildren, in various activities such as experimental reconstruction. These children are building a kiln from wattle and daub.

CRUMBLING AWAY

Pollution is destroying our past and our future. Chemicals from industrial and domestic activities are badly damaging many structures that have stood for thousands of years. Car exhaust fumes are seriously corroding Greece's great monument, the Parthenon.

HERE TODAY, GONE TOMORROW

Relics of the past are being destroyed by roads, buildings, deep ploughing, and massive peatcutting. In many countries laws protect the past, and require surveys, recording, and often rescue excavation before construction begins. While individual sites can be protected, ancient landscapes are more difficult, being slowly destroyed by agriculture.

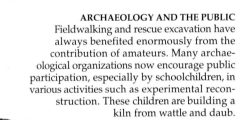

Excavator is rescuing vital information about Viking occupation

Rescue excavation at Roman and Viking York in England

Index

Acknowledgements

**Dorling Kindersley would like
to thank:**

The British Museum, especially Ivor
Kerslake for his efficient organization of
the photography, and Peter Hayman,
Chas Howson, Tony Milton, Nick
Nicholls, Mike Row, and Trevor
Springett for special photography;
and for help on research Janet Ambers,
Caroline Cartwright, Angela Evans,
Dr. Anne Farrer, Loretta Hogan, Simon
James, Janet Larkin, Dr. Andrew Oddy,
Allyson Rae, Jeffrey Spencer, Judith
Swaddling, Jonathan Tubb, David
Williams, and Helen Wolfe.
For help on research and photography:
Peter Reynolds, Copper Hastings,
Edward Perry, Simon Harlow, and Dave
Kirby at Butser Ancient Farm;
Dr. Francis Pryor, Maisie Taylor, Janet
Neve, Andy Dale, Toby Fox, and Bob

Woodward at Flag Fen Excavations;
Kathy Tubb at The Institute of
Archaeology (University of London);
Dr. David de Haan, Katie Foster, and
Marilyn Higson at The Ironbridge Gorge
Museum; Dr. Margaret Rule, Andrew
Elkerton, Alex Hildred, Richard
Hubbard, Maggie Richards, and Sue
James at The Mary Rose Trust; John
Chase (photography), Gavin Morgan,
Barry Gray, Jenny Hall, and Cheryl
Thorogood at The Museum of London;
Joslyn McDiarmid of Grosvenor Prints;
and Mike Dunning, Lynton Gardiner,
Colin Keates, Dave King, James
Stephenson, Harry Taylor, and Michael
Zabé for extra photography.
For design and editorial assistance:
Sarah Cowley, Ivan Finnegan, Kati
Poynor, Sharon Spencer, Helena Spiteri,
Susan St. Louis, and Isaac Zamora.

Picture credits
t=top b=bottom c=centre l-left r=right

Ancient Art & Architecture: 50bc, 53tr.
Archaeological Resource Centre: 63cr.
Bridgeman Art Library: 10tc.
British Museum: 14–15, 15c, 16cl, 16br,
17c, 20–21, 26cl, 26cr, 27br, 40bl, 40bc,
41cbr, 51b/Jonathan Tubb: 22cl, 22bl,
22bc, 23tc, 23tr, 23cr, 24tr, 24cr, 24b, 36c.
Bruce Coleman: 16bc/Nigel Blythe
Photography: 18b/Trevor Barrett:
16tl/John Cancalosi: 16tr.
Comstock: 12bl.
C. M. Dixon: 30cl, 30tr, 31l, 31cr, 31br,
42bc.
Mary Evans: 11bc, 60tl.
E. T. Archive: 11br, 14b.
Flag Fen Trust: 37cr.
Jo Flood: 45ctr.
Werner Forman Archive: 29br, 53cl.
Kenneth Garrett: 13b, 42tl, 42cr, 43b.
Mike Gorman/Scott Polar Research
Institute: 12cl.
Robert Harding Picture Library: 6–7b,

8cl, 62–63, 63cl.
Michael Holford: 21tl, 27tr, 57tr.
IBM/UK Ltd.: 53crt, 53crb.
INAH/Mexican Museum Authority
15b.
Mary Rose Trust: 6bl, 9br, 32tr, 33cl,
33cr, 34clt, 34clb, 34c, 34tr, 35r.
The Master and Fellows, Magdalene
College, Cambridge: 32cl.
Museum of London: 9tr.
Novosti: 30br.
Roger Palmer: 12c, 12cr, 22br.
Axel Poignant Archive: 44bc.
Tom Rasmussen: 21cr.
Chris Scarre: 47cbr.
Science Museum 60ct.
Science Photo Library/Alfred Pasieka:
62br.
Suffolk County Council: 26tr.
Sutton Hoo Research Trust/Martin
Carver: 43tr.
Dr. Martin Waller: 47b.
York Archaeological Trust: 6c, 10c, 46bl,
63b.
Michael Zabé 13t.

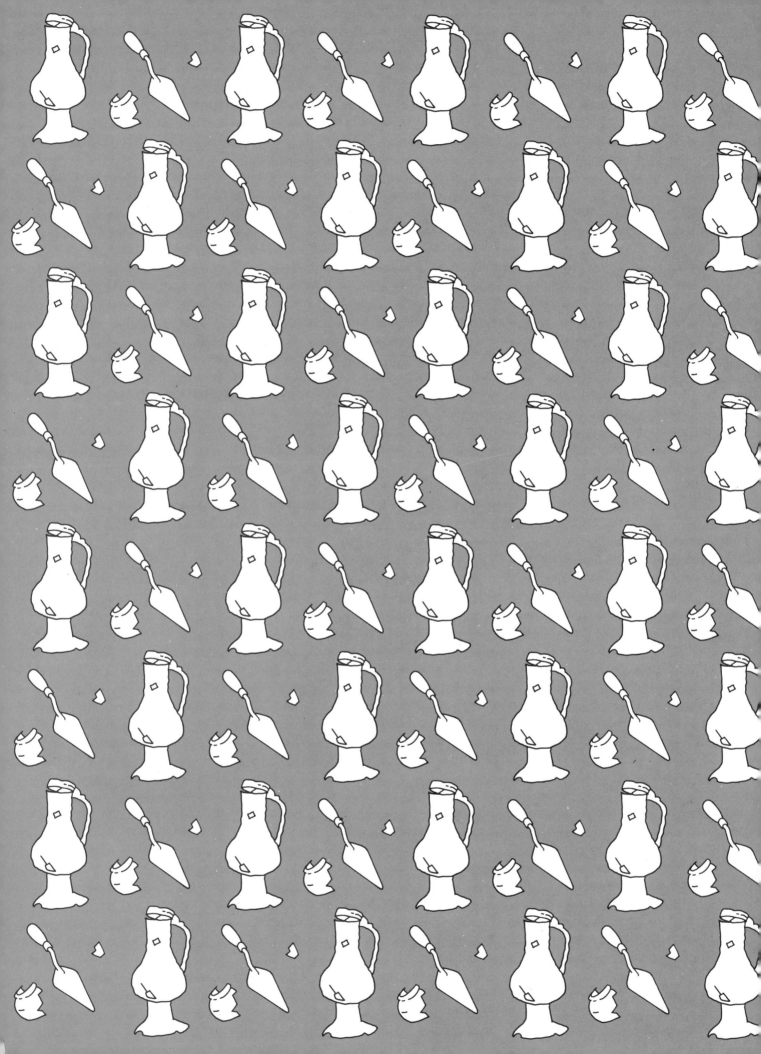